W9-AZG-893

MYSTIC SEAPORT

A Visitor's Guide

Mystic Seaport
75 Greenmanville Ave., P.O. Box 6000
Mystic, CT 06355-0990

www.mysticseaport.org

© 2005 by Mystic Seaport Museum, Inc.
All rights reserved
Manufactured in the United States of America

Text by Andrew W. German, with the assistance of Elysa Engelman,
Glenn Gordinier, Michael O'Farrell, William Peterson, Jonathan Shay,
Rick Spencer, and Cherie Sweeney

Photography by Kathleen Ramey Gilman, Judy Beisler, Kane Borden,
Oliver Denison III, Nancy d'Estang, Peter Fix, Bill Grant,
Dennis A. Murphy, Mary Anne Stets, Don Treworgy, and
Claire White-Peterson

ISBN 0-939510-79-0

CONTENTS

BEFORE YOU BEGIN YOUR VISIT

- A visit to Mystic Seaport can last as long as you wish. Plan on several hours to see the highlights and a day or more to see every exhibit. Your admission ticket is good for two days if you have it validated before leaving. A membership allows you unlimited visits each year.

- If you have limited time, don't miss the Museum's signature exhibit, *Voyages: Stories of America and the Sea*, in the Stillman Building, #46 on your map. Also, don't fail to board the *Charles W. Morgan* (#33), the last surviving American sailing whaleship, and the fishing schooner *L.A. Dunton* (#4). The Mystic River Scale Model (#7) will show you what the Mystic River looked like during the height of the shipbuilding industry here in the 1800s. Other highlights include the Shipsmith Shop (#22), which usually has a smith at work, the figurehead exhibit in the Wendell Building (#47), and the Preservation Shipyard (#2), where the Museum maintains and restores its historic vessels.

- Shirts and shoes must be worn at all times. Because a visit involves a good deal of walking over the uneven surfaces of our historic village and vessels, comfortable shoes will make your visit most enjoyable. If you tire of walking, there are many benches located around the Museum grounds.

- Leashed pets are welcome, but they may not enter Museum buildings or vessels. Please pick up after your pet, and do not leave pets unattended.

- Mystic Seaport buildings and vessels are smoke free.

- Food and beverages are not permitted in exhibit buildings or on board vessels. State law prohibits bringing alcohol to the Museum. For your convenience, beer, wine, and liquor are for sale in designated areas.

- Visitors are welcome to photograph, videotape, sketch, or otherwise record images of Mystic Seaport for personal use only. All other use is an infringement of the Museum's intellectual property and is prohibited and strictly enforced. Flash photography and tripods are not allowed in exhibit buildings or on board vessels. The Museum's Communications Office is available to work with authors, photographers, and the press for news and commercial purposes.

- Please turn cell phones and pagers to silent mode while on the Museum grounds. Phone conversations should be conducted at a discrete distance from programs and exhibits.

- Should you have a problem, including lost children, lost possessions, and health issues, the Museum's security force is here to assist you. The security office faces the Village Green, behind Stone's General Store (#38). Any Museum staff member can help you contact a security officer.

- Many Museum exhibits are staffed by professional educators who will talk with you about details of their exhibit. Staffed exhibits are identified by a blue and yellow signal flag, which in the maritime code means "let's communicate!" You may also encounter a role player in period dress, who will talk to you of his or her life as if you were transported back to the 1870s.

⚑ MYSTIC SEAPORT ⚑

*A*s picturesque and well established as it looks, Mystic Seaport is an imaginary place. There never was a seaport on this site. But about 50 years after the Greenman shipyard ceased operations here, three local men founded an association to preserve the legacy of America's maritime connections. Their vision has grown into Mystic Seaport—The Museum of America and the Sea.

The man with the clearest vision was Carl C. Cutler, a lawyer from a seafaring family who had made a voyage under sail himself. In the 1920s Cutler was researching a book on American clipper ships, and as he traveled the East Coast in search of information he was appalled to discover how much history, in the form of manuscripts, models, and other artifacts of the 1700s and 1800s, was being destroyed as places lost their maritime connections. Charles K. Stillman, a New York doctor who had returned to Mystic to live in the house of his grandfather, shipbuilder Clark Greenman, agreed with Cutler. They enlisted Edward Bradley, a local silk manufacturer who had made a voyage to China as a teenager. The three began planning in the summer of 1929, and on Christmas Day that year they incorporated the Marine Historical Association, which would become Mystic Seaport.

With Bradley as the institution's first president, the three men began recruiting members and collecting maritime artifacts even before they had a location for their planned museum. In 1931, funds from a Greenman descendant helped the association buy the defunct textile mill originally built by the shipbuilding Greenmans. The wooden mill was torn down, and the brick buildings became the Museum's first exhibit halls. The first exhibit was opened for members in what is now the Wendell Building in September 1931. Earlier that year, Dr. Stillman gave the Museum its first boat, the sandbagger racing sloop *Annie*.

The public was first invited to visit the Museum in the summer of 1934, with one exhibit open on Thursday and Saturday afternoons. A second exhibit building opened in 1935, and the Stillman Building (now site of the Museum's signature *Voyages* exhibit) first opened in 1938.

As their museum grew slowly through the Great Depression, the three founders had great plans for expansion. In their efforts to collect historical material and to teach American values through history, they had much in common with the Rockefeller family, who began to restore Colonial Williamsburg in the 1920s, with Henry Ford, who began his museum and Greenfield Village about the same time, and with the Wells family, who founded Old Sturbridge Village. Carl Cutler believed the nation could learn much from the example of heartily self-reliant New England seafarers. Stillman foresaw a school where young people could learn courage, confidence, and skill through on-the-water experience. All three wished to bring actual ships to Mystic, so visitors could experience the full-scale reality of the story.

Both Stillman and Bradley died in 1938, but Cutler took over as managing director and began to realize their dreams. Searching for an appropriate ship, he negotiated acquisition of the

The training ship *Joseph Conrad* joined the fleet by act of Congress in 1947 as a first step in the planned Mariner Training Program that began on board in 1949. With the arrival of the coasting schooner *Australia* in 1951 and the schooner yacht *Brilliant* in 1952, the sail training program expanded, with the *Brilliant* taking groups of sea scouts on week-long coastal cruises.

whaleship *Charles W. Morgan*, the last of her kind, which had been displayed near her home port of New Bedford, Massachusetts, until she was damaged in the 1938 hurricane and left without financial support. The ship arrived in November 1941, just a month before the attack on Pearl Harbor brought the U.S. into World War II. She was placed in a sand berth and opened for visitors in June 1942. Even in the middle of the war, the institution grew as visitors and service people came here for inspiration. The plan to build a representative seaport began to take shape in 1943. The first building to arrive was the shipsmith shop, which was moved to the Museum in 1944.

The Museum flourished during the years of postwar patriotism and prosperity. By 1948 the term "Mystic Seaport" was being used for the growing outdoor museum on the bank of the Mystic River. Membership in the institution had increased from 27 in 1930 to 500 in 1945 and more than 1,000 in 1947. Annual visitation grew from about 180 in 1935 to more than 6,000 during the war years and 23,000 in 1947.

With the grounds stabilized behind stone bulkheads, the waterfront street took shape through the 1950s as buildings were moved in or built. In 1955, "activists"—now called interpreters—began to work in the exhibits, explaining them to visitors. By the late 1950s the Museum had 6,000 members and was hosting a quarter of a million visitors a year. More than 1,000 private boats tied up at the Museum's piers in July and August 1956. To preserve the period flavor of the site, the parking lot was moved from the present site of the Village Green to locations across the street from the growing Museum grounds.

Despite the emphasis on visitors, the Museum was never simply a tourist attraction. As early as 1930 it had published its first of many monographs. The growing collection of books and manuscripts was finally deposited in a small library in 1947, and this library served as the center for the graduate-level Frank C. Munson

Memorial Institute of American Maritime History, which has been held at the Museum every summer since 1955. School group visitation and staff visits to schools have also been an important form of educational outreach since the early 1950s.

The 1960s saw even greater expansion at Mystic Seaport. The

Planetarium was opened in 1960, the Seamen's Inne was opened in 1964 to offer formal dining at the Museum, and in 1965 the new Mildred C. Mallory Memorial Membership Building, the G.W. Blunt White Library, and the expanded Museum store were opened. In 1964, the year the fishing schooner *L.A. Dunton* joined the Museum's fleet, almost 3,000 boats called at the Museum and nearly 350,000 people visited. The completion of the nearby interstate highway 95 offered convenient access for visitors from the major markets between New York and Boston. By 1968—the year the Museum was featured in *National Geographic Magazine*—more than half a million visitors arrived.

With such success came concerns about overextension, especially as the growing fleet of large vessels exceeded the Museum's ability to care for them. The small shipyard and marine railway set up in 1957 could not keep up with the needed work. The *Australia* was hauled ashore for work in 1961 and never returned to the water. Other vessels were passed on to other organizations, such as the Arctic exploration schooner *Bowdoin*, purchased in 1959 and sold in 1968.

To keep up with the demands of its wooden fleet, the Museum made a major commitment to the preservation of its ships. With expert guidance and the firm direction of Waldo C.M. Johnston, it planned and built the Henry B. duPont Preservation Shipyard on filled land at the site of the historic Charles Mallory shipyard at the south side of the Museum grounds. The first major task for the new Preservation Shipyard, the first of its kind, was to restore the National Historic Landmark *Charles W. Morgan*, which was pulled from her sand berth and refloated in December 1973.

The successful restoration of this ship signaled a new mission for the Museum: the preservation of skills as well as artifacts. This effort included the new Special Demonstration Squad, created to engage visitors in some traditional maritime skills, such as sail-handling. The shipyard needed skilled shipwrights, so it became a center for both experienced shipbuilders and young people eager to learn. With the arrival of John Gardner, the Museum widened its emphasis on traditional wooden small craft and began to offer boatbuilding and boat-handling classes. And maritime skills and seagoing experience were integral parts of the academically rigorous undergraduate Williams College-Mystic Seaport Maritime Studies Program established at the Museum in 1977.

The Museum's attendance reached an all-time high in the bicentennial year of 1976. In the decades since, all outdoor museums have faced challenges as both the pace of work and the range of leisure-time pursuits have increased for Americans. Mystic Seaport continued to refine itself through the 1980s, building new bulkheads along its waterfront, improving visitor access, and expanding its collections, notably with the acquisition of the Rosenfeld Collection of maritime photographs, which numbers close to a million images.

Long viewed as a quaintly New England museum, Mystic Seaport redefined itself as The Museum of America and the Sea in the 1990s. The construction of the Freedom Schooner *Amistad* in the Preservation Shipyard in 1998-2000 was an acclaimed part of this more inclusive mission. That same year, the Museum opened its signature exhibit, *Voyages: Stories of America and the Sea*. With the opening of the new Collections Research Center in 2001, the Museum began to manage its intellectual property in new ways that will make it both a destination and presence far beyond Mystic.

Now in its eighth decade, Mystic Seaport continues to engage visitors with the mystique of human connections with the sea. Continually evolving, yet forever tied to the traditions of American seafaring that so long ago inspired the vision of its founders, this is Mystic Seaport—The Museum of America and the Sea.

MYSTIC

THE MUSEUM OF

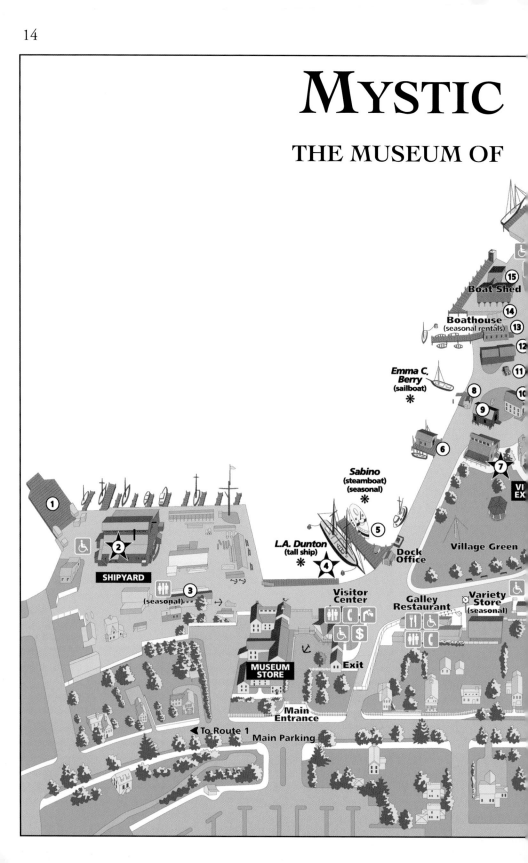

Boat Shed (15)

Boathouse (14)
(seasonal rentals) (13)

(12)

(11)

Emma C. Berry (sailboat)
✳

(8)

(10)

(9)

(6)

(7)

Sabino (steamboat) (seasonal)
✳

VI EX

(1)

L.A. Dunton (tall ship)
✳

(5)

Dock Office

(4)

Village Green

(2)

SHIPYARD

(3)
(seasonal)

Visitor Center

Galley Restaurant

Variety Store (seasonal)

$

MUSEUM STORE

Exit

Main Entrance

◀ To Route 1   **Main Parking**

SEAPORT

AMERICA AND THE SEA®

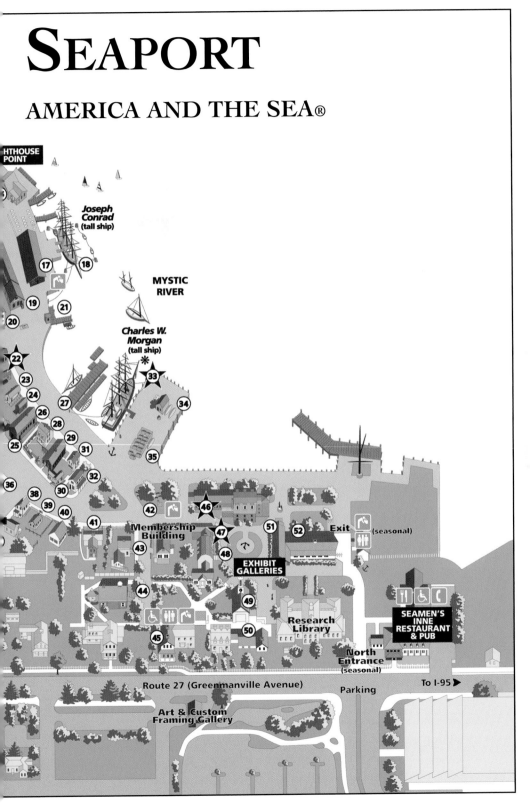

HTHOUSE POINT

Joseph Conrad (tall ship)

17　18

19　21

20

MYSTIC RIVER

Charles W. Morgan (tall ship)

22

23

24

27

26

28

29

31

25

32

33

34

35

36

38　30

39

40

41

42　46

Membership Building

47

43

48

EXHIBIT GALLERIES

51　52　Exit　(seasonal)

44

49

Research Library

SEAMEN'S INNE RESTAURANT & PUB

45

50

North Entrance (seasonal)

Route 27 (Greenmanville Avenue)　Parking　To I-95 ▶

Art & Custom Framing Gallery

1,2 HENRY B. DUPONT PRESERVATION SHIPYARD

Mystic Seaport's Preservation Shipyard is a unique, world-famous facility with the equipment and skilled workers needed to maintain, restore, and preserve the Museum's vessels. As they did when in service, the Museum's vessels require regular work, and the Shipyard staff of about 20, who are skilled with both hand and power tools, ensures that the work is done to the highest standards.

Completed in 1972 on the approximate site occupied by the Charles Mallory Shipyard more than 100 years earlier, the Museum's

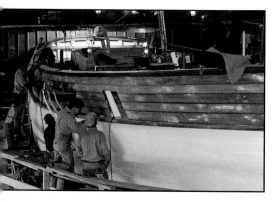

pine, and hackmatack; and a sawmill. With its moving truck and three blades, the sawmill can accommodate logs 40 feet long and up to four feet thick. Nearby is a 1930s Fay & Eagan shipsaw, a large bandsaw with a tilting head to cut the changing bevels often required in large ship timbers.

Research and documentation are essential to the work of preservation and restoration of our exhibit vessels. The Shipyard Documentation Shop conducts research for restoration proj-

Preservation Shipyard consists of a large main shop where a visitor's gallery overlooks carpenters' shops, an 85-foot spar lathe, a rigging loft, and a large open area where vessels are brought indoors for repair.

The Preservation Shipyard also includes a paint shop for painting and varnishing; a metal-working shop; a lumber shed for seasoning and storage of traditional shipbuilding timbers like white oak, live oak, yellow pine, white

ects and keeps detailed records and photos of each project.

Central to the shipyard is a 375-ton-capacity lift dock capable of raising any of the Museum's ships out of the water for repair or maintenance. The lift dock was completed in 1973, just in time to haul the 350-ton whaleship *Charles W. Morgan* after she was removed from her sand berth after 30 years. All of the Museum's vessels have been on the lift dock for major restoration as well as routine maintenance. The dock is raised and lowered about one foot per minute by 16 cables that run through pulley blocks and are wound around drums powered by a 100-horsepower electric motor. In the next few years the Museum will install an updated design.

KINGSTON II
HARBOR TUG

Mystic Seaport has its own tugboat to move its vessels to and from the Shipyard, to turn them annually, and to do other big jobs along the waterfront. She is also outfitted as a fireboat. Originally built in 1937 at the Electric Boat shipyard in Groton, Connecticut, the 44-foot Kingston II is thought to have been one of the earliest all-welded vessels. She was built from scrap steel by apprentice welders and spent more than 40 years moving submarines at the Electric Boat yard before her donation to the Museum by the General Dynamics Corporation in 1980.

AMISTAD

With construction funds from the State of Connecticut, the 80-foot Freedom Schooner Amistad was built in the Preservation Shipyard between 1998 and 2000. She is a reproduction of a trading schooner that figured in a revolt by African captives off Cuba in 1839, which resulted in a U.S. Supreme Court case and the eventual return of the captives to Africa. The vessel's mission, to teach lessons of history, leadership, and cooperation between

races, was realized during her construction and continues through her travels and her education prog Operated by Amistad America, a nonprofit educational organization, the Amistad is sometimes berthed at I Seaport between voyages.

Marine Engines

Several examples of marine engines are displayed in the Shipyard. The largest is the 14-foot-high compound steam engine from the New York Harbor tugboat Socony 5, built in 1927. Developed about 1870, the two-cylinder compound engine had a small high-pressure cylinder into which the steam was first directed. After expanding to drive the piston, the steam was exhausted into the larger low-pressure cylinder, where it expanded further to drive the second piston. This 850-horsepower engine turned a 10-foot propeller.

At sea, oil engines replaced steam engines in the first half of the 1900s. The high-compression crude-oil engine was developed by Rudolph Diesel and began to be used at sea after 1910. Safe, long-running, and powerful, the crude-oil engine today powers anything from a 30-foot yacht to a 1,000-foot containership.

Two marine diesels have been restored and are occasionally run in the Shipyard. Built in Norway in the 1930s, the 83-horsepower Wichmann semi-diesel was acquired by the Museum and restored in the 1990s.

The 90-horsepower Lathrop diesel was built just down the Mystic River by the Lathrop Engine Company in the late 1940s. Founded in 1897, the Lathrop company built marine gasoline engines before adding safer diesel engines to its line in the 1920s. These engines remained popular among fishermen and yachtsmen until the 1950s. When the Museum acquired it in 1985, this engine had only a few hours of service. Volunteers restored it to operation in the 1990s.

3 *THAMES* KEEL AND SHIPBUILDING EXHIBIT

The 92-foot keel assembly from the whaleship *Thames* is set up on blocks in a shed within the Preservation Shipyard. The keel is the "backbone" and the starting point for the construction of a ship. Displayed along the entire length of the keel is an exhibit on the process of shipbuilding that takes visitors from keel laying to launching.

Built in 1818 on the Connecticut River at Essex, the *Thames* was first a two-masted brig but was later rerigged as a three-masted ship. During an 1822 whaling voyage from New Haven to the Pacific, she delivered a company of missionaries to the Hawaiian Islands. She then made 11 whaling voyages to the South Atlantic from Sag Harbor, Long Island. She ended her days scuttled as a breakwater in Sag Harbor after being condemned in 1838. About 1930 the ship was dynamited in order to recover the copper with which it was sheathed and fastened. These timbers were rediscovered in 1968 during construction of a marina. After Saltair Industries gave them to the Museum in 1971, the keel was set up in this exhibit. Nearby are mock-ups of a ship's framing and planking, to explain the wooden shipbuilding process.

Outside is the enormous trunk of a live oak tree that grew on John's Island, South Carolina, for 600 years before it was toppled by Hurricane Hugo in 1989. Its long branches have been used for ship timber. The burn marks on the trunk are thought to date from the time of slavery, when the tree was a gathering place.

RESOLUTE
LAUNCH

In the warmer months, for a small fee you can take a ride along the Mystic Seaport waterfront in the classic power launch *Resolute*, which was designed and built by the renowned Herreshoff Manufacturing Company yacht-building yard in Bristol, Rhode Island. Launched about 1917 for possible U.S. Navy use, this 26-foot boat served as the tender for the America's Cup defender *Resolute* in 1920. She then became a launch at the Seawanhaka Corinthian Yacht Club on Long Island, ferrying members and visitors between their boats and shore. Acquired by the Museum in 1980, she was restored to continue her service as a passenger launch.

ANNIE
CLASS A RACING SANDBAGGER

The first craft to be acquired by Mystic Seaport, and one of the most notable on display, is the Mystic-built sandbagger sloop *Annie*. The *Annie* is a centerboard racing sloop of a type popular between 1865 and 1896. The base of her sail plan measures more than twice the length of the boat; the *Annie* herself is only 29 feet long, but overall it is nearly 70 feet from the end of her bowsprit to the tip of her boom. Adapted from wide, shallow New York oyster boats, these sloops raced in classes based on length alone, so skippers could carry as much sail as they dared. To keep from capsizing, a crew of 14 men balanced the *Annie*'s 1,313 square feet of sail with their own weight and with 1,500 pounds of sandbags, which they shifted each time the boat tacked. Reflecting their movable ballast, these extreme sailboats came to be known as sandbaggers.

"The finest helmsmanship ever seen was that practiced on a sandbagger. On this type for hours at a time, this vessel was kept on her feet solely by the skillful handling of the helm. She was driven along just on the edge of her stability, and the least uncertainty of movement, the slightest hesitation, meant a capsize, wrote boating authority Thomas Day."

Born in an era when professional watermen and amateurs competed together, sandbagger racing spread from New York to Long Island Sound, Philadelphia, New Orleans, and the West Coast. Large crowds watched the races, with many spectators betting on their favorite boats. But as yacht clubs adopted sandbagger racing in the 1870s, professionals were prohibited from competing and boats began to be measured. With the prohibition against movable ballast in 1896, sandbagger racing came to an end.

Built by D.O. Richmond on the west bank of the Mystic River in 1880, the *Annie* was owned by Henry H. Tift of Mystic and Tifton, Georgia, and raced successfully in eastern Long Island Sound and during the winter in Georgia and Florida. Like many sandbaggers, she was converted for fishing or oystering when her racing career was over. Acquired by Mystic Seaport in 1931, she was the first boat in the Museum's collection. She has been extensively rebuilt several times throughout her existence, most recently in 2000-04.

The *Annie* under sail, ca. 1890. (Mystic Seaport 1949.843)

WHAT RIG IS THAT?

The arrangement of masts and sails on sailing vessels has a language all its own. Here are a few terms to help you identify what you see along the waterfront at Mystic Seaport.

Bark (or barque)—a vessel with at least three masts, having square-rigged sails on the forward masts and a fore-and-aft rig on the aftermost (mizzen) mast. The *Charles W. Morgan* is rigged as a bark, giving her slightly more maneuverability, and requiring a smaller crew, than did her original ship rig.

Boom—the horizontal spar at the foot of a fore-and-aft sail.

Bowsprit—the horizontal spar extending forward from the bow of a vessel to provide a better angle of support for the stays that hold up the foremast.

Brig—a two-masted, square-rigged vessel. Other than models, the Museum does not have a brig in its collection, but occasionally a brig-rigged yacht or training vessel visits the Museum.

Catboat—a single-masted, fore-and-aft-rigged vessel with the mast stepped at the very bow and having only one sail. The Cape Cod Catboat *Breck Marshall* is one of many catboats in the Museum's watercraft collection.

Fore-and-aft rig—an arrangement of sails in which the leading edge (luff) of each sail attaches to the mast, placing the plane of the sail aft of the mast. Since a fore-and-aft sail works something like the wing of an airplane, this rig is most efficient for sailing toward the direction from which the wind blows.

Foremast—if a vessel has at least two masts, it's the forward one, unless it's the larger of the two, in which case it's called the mainmast.

Gaff rig—a form of four-sided fore-and-aft sail having an angled spar called the gaff to support the head. Until the introduction of the triangular "marconi" sail in the 1920s, this was the standard form of fore-and-aft sail for catboats, schooners, and sloops.

Jib—a triangular fore-and-aft sail set on one of the stays in front of a vessel's forwardmost mast. Depending on their locations, jibs have different proper names. Similar sails called staysails may also be set on the stays between masts.

Ketch—a two-masted, fore-and-aft-rigged vessel in which the after (mizzen) mast is shorter than the forward (main) mast and is stepped in front of the helm or rudder (if it's set behind, the rig is called a yawl). In summer, the ketch *Araminta* is often on her mooring near Chubb's Wharf.

Mainmast—the largest mast in a multimasted vessel. Usually it is the second, or it is the larger of two.

Mizzenmast—the aftermost mast when a vessel has three or, in a two-masted vessel, when the forward mast is taller.

Ratlines—the ropes hitched to a vessel's stays to make a ladder for the crew to use.

Running rigging—the many lines used to operate a vessel's sails, including halyards to raise sails, sheets to trim fore-and-aft sails, braces to trim square sails, and many other specialized lines. For mechanical advantage, running rigging usually runs through blocks (pulleys).

Schooner—a vessel with at least two masts (the foremast being no larger than the others), having fore-and-aft sails on all masts. If the foremast is taller, the vessel is a ketch or a yawl. Fishing schooners normally had two masts, like the Museum's *L.A. Dunton*. As cargo schooners increased in size, up to 300 feet long, the number of masts increased to six, and in one case seven. At 70 feet, the Museum's coasting schooner *Australia* had two masts.

Ship—we may call any large vessel a ship, but technically a sailing ship has at least three masts, all of them square-rigged. The *Joseph Conrad* is rigged as a ship.

Sloop—a single-masted, fore-and-aft-rigged vessel with at least one triangular jib set in front of the mast. The Museum has many sloops in its watercraft collection, both working vessels like the *Emma C. Berry*, and yachts like the *Vireo*.

Square rig—an arrangement of sails in which they are hung from horizontal yards attached to the masts so the plane of the sails is approximately at right angles to the length of the vessel. In contrast to the fore-and-aft rig, the square rig is designed to be pushed by the wind. The yards can be swung (braced) about 45 degrees in each direction to change the vessel's orientation to the wind, but a square-rigger cannot sail close to the wind or maneuver easily.

Standing rigging—the many lines called stays that support a vessel's masts. The standing rigging of the Museum's vessels is mostly made of wire rope that has been parceled (wrapped in canvas) and served (wrapped tightly with yarns called marline) before being tarred to protect it from the effects of water.

Topsail schooner—a two-masted, fore-and-aft-rigged vessel having square sails on its foremast. The *Amistad* is a topsail schooner.

Yards—the horizontal spars that support the sails in a square-rigged vessel. The tips of the yards are called yardarms.

4 *L.A. DUNTON* FISHING SCHOONER

Between 1865 and 1930, New England fishermen relied on many-hooked trawl lines set from open boats called dories to catch cod and other bottom-dwelling fish that thrived on the shallow banks of the continental shelf. In big schooners like the *L.A. Dunton*, the fishermen worked in two-man teams as dorymates, forming a bond of trust on which their very lives depended.

The *L.A. Dunton* represents the final form of the sailing schooners that served as mother ship for a fleet of ten or more dories used by the fishermen to set and haul their lines. These schooners combined the best features of earlier designs: *speed* to rush the catch to port for a good price at market; *maneuverability* to tend their dories at sea and to sail into the prevailing southwest winds on the way home; and *stability* to endure the high winds and heavy seas on the banks, especially during the winter fishing season.

Designed by Thomas F. McManus, the most prolific designer of fishing schooners, the 123-foot vessel was built by Arthur D. Story and launched from his well-known yard at Essex, Massachusetts, in 1921. Built after auxiliary engines had become common

in schooners, the *Dunton* was probably the last large engineless fishing schooner.

Captain Felix J. Hogan owned and commanded the *L.A. Dunton* from 1921 to 1932. Like the majority of New England dorymen, Hogan was an immigrant, coming from his native Newfoundland as a young man to find

On the Banks

On the continental shelf, between the warm waters of the Gulf Stream and the cold flow of the Labrador Current, shallow plateaus called banks are fertile grounds for marine life. For more than 500 years, fishermen have come to the banks seeking the natural bounty of cod, haddock, halibut, and other edible fish. Sailing from the principal New England fishing ports of Gloucester and Boston, the L.A. Dunton worked all these waters, from Georges Bank 100 miles east of Cape Cod, to the Grand Bank of Newfoundland, 800 miles east-northeast of Gloucester.

When New England fishermen began to work shallow, rough Georges Bank in the 1830s, it was the most productive fishing bank in the North Atlantic. The L.A. Dunton usually fished these waters between Labor Day and Easter, catching haddock, cod, hake, cusk, pollock, and halibut to be sold fresh in Boston. By the end of the Dunton's American career in the early 1930s the effects of overfishing on Georges had been noticed, but the fishing effort increased. The net form of fishing represented by the Museum's eastern-rig dragger Roann, practiced through the 1960s and 1970s by huge foreign fishing ships as well as U.S. and Canadian vessels, depleted the most popular species. In 1994, most of Georges Bank was closed to fishing in hopes that the haddock, cod, and flounder populations would recover.

better pay and living conditions in Gloucester schooners. A fun-loving skipper who played cards with his crew and was known for dancing the jig, Hogan earned the respect of his fishermen by finding fish and using good judgment at sea. Under his command, the *Dunton* usually fished for haddock in winter and halibut in summer, ranging from Georges Bank off Cape Cod to the Grand Banks off Newfoundland. She averaged about 18 voyages a year, usually packing the fish in ice and landing them fresh in Boston. By 1923 she was equipped with a 100-horsepower Fairbanks, Morse crude-oil engine. Though she met her share of bad weather, the *Dunton* never lost a man.

When he retired from fishing during the Great Depression, Felix Hogan sold the *L.A. Dunton* to new owners in Newfoundland. As an engine-powered vessel with shortened masts and a pilothouse to shelter her wheel, the *Dunton*

The *L.A. Dunton* on the fishing grounds. (Mystic Seaport 1964-2-28)

A Doryman's Day

If you were one of the L.A. Dunton's 20 fishermen, this might be your daily schedule during a voyage lasting between one and six weeks:

3:00 A.M., cook gets up to start breakfast

4:00, you and the rest of the fishermen get up and drink a cup of coffee

4:15-5:30, you and your dorymate each bait 750-1,000 hooks

5:30-6:30, leaving the captain and cook to sail the schooner, you and your dorymate row out in your dory and set more than a mile of trawl line

6:30-7:30, back on board, breakfast is served in two shifts; one of you eats while the other works on gear, then switch

8:30-10:00, you and your dorymate row out in your dory and haul the trawl, hoping you've caught as many as 2,000 fish

10:00-11:30, returning to the schooner, you and the rest of the fishermen clean the morning's catch and pack the fish in the hold

11:30 A.M.-12:30 P.M., dinner is served in two shifts; one of you eats while the other baits; then switch

12:30-1:30, leaving the captain and cook to sail the schooner, you and your dorymate row out in your dory and set more than a mile of trawl line

1:30-3:00, back on board, you have a mug-up (snack) and work on fishing gear

3:00-4:30, you and your dorymate row out in your dory and haul the trawl, hoping you've caught as many as 2,000 fish

4:30-6:00, you and the rest of the fishermen clean the afternoon's catch and pack the fish in the hold

6:00-7:00, supper, served in two shifts; one of you eats while the other baits (if another set is planned) or cleans up gear, then switch

7:00-11:00, if the captain calls for another set you and your dorymate row out in your dory and set the trawl, then haul it, clean the evening's catch, and pack the fish in the hold. Otherwise, you are free to rest, play cards or music, or tell stories

11:00, if you are lucky you turn into your bunk for five hours of sleep, but if the weather turns bad you may all be called out to take in sail

12:00-2:00 A.M., every few evenings, you and your dorymate are called for your two-hour watch on deck, one of you at the wheel, the other on lookout at the bow

fished the Grand Banks for another 20 years. She carried at least one cargo of salt cod across the Atlantic to Portugal and returned with salt. The *L.A. Dunton* became a coastal freighter in 1955 and was purchased for preservation by Mystic Seaport in 1963.

Soon after the *Dunton*'s arrival, the Museum began to restore her to her original design. Then, between 1974 and 1985, Museum shipwrights removed her engine, restored her stern to the correct appearance, replaced deck beams, deck planking, and frames, and replanked her topsides. Ongoing restoration maintains the *Dunton,* one of the few surviving New England fishing schooners, as a testimonial to the hardworking fishermen who manned her. The *L.A. Dunton* was designated a National Historic Landmark in 1994.

How Does the *Sabino*'s Engine Work?

Steam is produced in a watertube boiler, in which the water circulates through the fire box in a series of tubes to produce high-pressure steam. Valves direct the steam first to the small high-pressure cylinder and from there to the larger low-pressure cylinder to expand against the pistons and drive the cranks that turn the propeller shaft. Her screw propeller—a maritime innovation of the 1840s—is far more efficient than the side 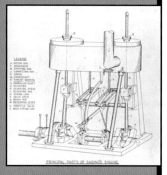 wheels that used to drive steamboats. Where does the steam go? After leaving the low-pressure cylinder it passes through a condenser pipe on the outside of the Sabino's hull, where it is cooled back to a liquid and pumped back into the boiler to go through the process again.

5 *SABINO* PASSENGER STEAMBOAT

From about 1820 to 1940, coastal and riverside residents relied on steamboats as much as we do on

cars and busses for convenient transportation. With poor roads and few bridges, it took far longer to travel on land than it did at eight miles an hour in a comfortable steamboat. But by 1900 the railroad had reduced the demand for steamboat service, and with the popularization of the automobile and the development of reliable paved highways in the 1920s, the steamboat became obsolete.

The 56-foot steamboat *Sabino* is the last remaining wooden, coalfired steamboat in operation in the U.S. Built in 1908 in East Boothbay, Maine, by W. Irving Adams, she spent most of her career ferrying passengers and cargo between Maine towns and islands. First she operated on the Damariscotta River in midcoast

Maine. After sinking during an accident in 1918, she ran on the Kennebec River. From 1927 to 1960 she served the islands of Casco Bay, running out of Portland. For this service her narrow hull was widened with sponsons to make her more stable in the open

waters. But though her configuration and passenger capacity changed through the years, her engine did not. She is still powered by the Paine compound—two-cylinder—steam engine installed in 1908; the present boiler was installed in 1940.

After being restored by the Corbin family of Newburyport, Massachusetts, the *Sabino* was purchased in 1974 to serve as a working exhibit at Mystic Seaport. She is operated during the warmer months on regularly scheduled runs for the enjoyment and education of visitors. In the 1980s and 1990s, the *Sabino* underwent major restorations to hull and engine in the Museum's Preservation Shipyard, making her sound as she approaches her second century of operation. The *Sabino* was formally designated a National Historic Landmark in 1992.

Newbert & Wallace Shipyard Privy

This simple shed at the end of the wharf between the *L. A. Dunton* and *Sabino* served as the toilet for shipwrights at the shipyard established by Herbert Newbert and Leroy Wallace in 1942. The yard specialized in building fishing vessels, including the Museum's eastern-rig dragger Roann. This one-hole privy, complete with ship carpenters' notations on its interior walls, represents the most basic form of sewage treatment used by Americans for centuries.

In Thomaston, Maine, the St. George River flushed the waste from the Newbert & Wallace yard. The Mystic River also served as a sewer for human and industrial waste from shipyards, shoreside businesses, and homes. Vessels also discharged their sewage overboard. Eventually, the water quality around many coastal communities was so degraded that marine life declined and human health suffered.

Beginning in 1972, the U.S. Congress passed a series of acts and amendments commonly known as the Clean Water Act, for "the protection and propagation of fish, shellfish, and wildlife and recreation in and on the water." The act authorized the Environmental Protection Agency to target "point source" pollution like untreated sewage. More recently, efforts have been aimed at eliminating runoff pollution and on maintaining the health of entire watersheds.

The Newbert & Wallace privy was brought to Mystic Seaport when a new flush toilet was installed at the yard in the early 1970s.

GERDA III
DANISH LIGHTHOUSE TENDER

Built in 1928 as a lighthouse tender, the *Gerda III* appears to be a common Danish workboat. But in October of 1943 she played a much more important role. The boat was used by Henny Søndig, the 19-year-old daughter of the boat's manager, and a four-man crew to rescue Jews from Nazi-occupied Denmark.

The refugees were brought to a warehouse along Copenhagen's waterfront and smuggled aboard the *Gerda III*, hiding in the cargo hold. The little vessel then set out on her official lighthouse supply duties, but detoured to the coast of neutral Sweden and put her "cargo" ashore. Although the vessel was regularly boarded and checked by German soldiers, the refugees were never discovered. The *Gerda III* rescued approximately 300 Jews, in groups of 10 to 15.

Henny Søndig and the brave crew were not part of the organized Danish resistance movement. Ordinary Danish citizens were outraged by the Nazi plan to deport Jews to the death camps. The Danish people mounted a spontaneous effort that saved more than 7,000 of their Jewish neighbors—almost the entire Jewish population of Denmark.

By an act of the Danish Parliament, the *Gerda III* was donated to The Museum of Jewish Heritage in New York City. The vessel was restored to her wartime appearance, complete with neutral flags, by the J. Ring Andersen yard in Denmark. Mystic Seaport is proud to help care for the boat and exhibit her in the United States.

ROANN
EASTERN-RIG DRAGGER

The *Roann* is one of the last surviving examples of the fishing vessels that replaced sailing schooners like the Museum's *L.A. Dunton*. As a dragger, she represents the revolutionary shift from sail to engine power and from hook-and-line to net for bottom fishing in New England. The otter trawl, a huge conical fishnet that is dragged across the bottom to sweep up fish, was developed in Europe and was introduced in New England around 1900. By the 1920s the otter trawl had superseded hook-and-line methods, and eastern-rig draggers were replacing schooners like the *Dunton* on the waterfront. Powered by a diesel engine, and dragging an otter trawl along the seabed, a dragger

like the 60-foot *Roann,* with a crew of three, could catch cod and haddock twice as fast as the *L.A. Dunton*'s dorymen could with their baited hooks. Draggers also were the first to catch large quantities of flounder.

As an "eastern-rig" vessel, the *Roann* has her pilothouse aft and her working deck amidships like the original draggers of eastern New England. This type of vessel had been introduced in New England about 25 years before the *Roann* herself was designed by Albert Condon in 1944 and built by Newbert & Wallace at Thomaston, Maine, in 1947. Roy Campbell—who combined his and his wife Ann's names to name his boat—fished the *Roann* out of Martha's Vineyard. In the 1960s Chet Westcott bought the boat and moved her to the fishing port of Point Judith, Rhode Island, and in the 1970s Tom Williams took over, fishing the boat with his sons.

In 1997 Tom Williams sold the boat to Mystic Seaport in order to buy one of the modern steel-hulled stern trawlers, successors to the eastern-rig draggers, which have their pilothouses forward and use net reels and stern ramps to fish more safely and even more productively. The Museum documented the boat's last fishing trip on film. The *Roann* was hauled at the Museum's Preservation Shipyard at the end of 2004 for a major restoration.

FLORENCE
WESTERN-RIG DRAGGER

As a western-rig dragger, the *Florence* represents a contrast to the eastern-rig dragger *Roann*. Along the southeastern shore of Connecticut, the smaller fishing boats adapted  for draggers evolved from sloops and catboats, having a broad aft deck for working and a small pilothouse forward. This arrangement became known as the "western rig."

The *Florence* was built in 1926, just down the Mystic River below the drawbridge, at the busy boatyard of Franklin G. Post. Her first engine was a 65 horsepower, 6-cylinder standard model built nearby by the Lathrop Engine Company, where Post had earlier worked. Under captains Morris Thompson and Howard Shaw she fished alongshore and out past Montauk Point and Block Island in search of flounder and cod. In summer she was sometimes used to catch surface-schooling mackerel and to hunt swordfish. She was being used to tend fish traps in Rhode Island when the Museum acquired her in 1982. She has been completely restored to her original configuration, including below-deck accommodations. She is powered by the Gray Marine 6-71 engine that served for much of her working life.

EMMA C. BERRY
CONNECTICUT SMACK

 One of the oldest surviving commercial vessels in America, the *Emma C. Berry* slid down the ways in June 1866 into the Mystic River at Noank, two miles south of Mystic at the mouth of the river. Built at the R. & J. Palmer shipyard by James A. Latham, the *Berry* was designed to the specifications of a Connecticut "smack"—an able design built throughout southeastern Connecticut and well known from Maine to the Caribbean. Captain John Henry Berry of Noank got what he asked for: a sloop rig carrying a large mainsail, two headsails and, for light weather, a gaff topsail. For storage of the catch, the vessel was equipped with a wet well, a large watertight compartment in the hold into which water flowed through numerous holes in the bottom hull planking, keeping the catch alive for delivery to market. Captain Berry named the smack for his daughter. Locally, the *Berry* fished for cod and mackerel, delivering them to market in New London, or even New York. Later, she was used to transport lobsters.

Rerigged as a schooner in 1886, taken to Maine in 1894, and fitted with a Knox gasoline engine in about 1916, the *Berry* was an active fisherman until 1924, when she was left on the flats at Beals Island, Maine. In 1926 Milton Beal bought her for use as a coastal freighter, sailing between Jonesport, Rockland, and Portland, Maine, and Gloucester, Massachusetts. In 1931 she was found and restored as a yacht by F. Slade Dale, a New Jersey yacht basin owner, who, in 1969, donated the *Berry* to Mystic Seaport. She has been restored twice at Mystic Seaport and was sailed in 1992 as a test of the performance of these handy fishing vessels. The *Emma C. Berry* was designated a National Historic Landmark in 1994.

6 THOMAS OYSTER HOUSE

In estuaries and shallow, protected waters along the American coast, oysters spawn and settle in dense natural beds. Except during the summer spawning months, Native American and then European fishermen worked these beds for sustenance and profit. Throughout the 1800s, oysters were extremely popular convenience food in cities from Boston to San Francisco. While Chesapeake Bay oysters, and later Gulf Coast oysters, were commonly canned, Long Island Sound oysters usually traveled to market either in their shells or else shucked—removed from their shells—and iced.

Research carried out in 1967 revealed that this structure is one of the few remaining northern oyster houses, where oyster boats unloaded their catch. Oysterman Thomas Thomas constructed the building about 1874 in the City Point section of New Haven, Connecticut, which once was the largest oyster distribution center in New England.

Thomas Thomas used the building as a culling shop, where oysters were sorted by size and shipped in their shells, by the barrel, to markets in New York City and as far away as California. Following Thomas Thomas's death, his son John took over the business and converted it to a shucking house. Although we do not know who worked there, we know that women began working as shuckers as early as the 1850s. Using a small hammer to break the tips of the shells and a knife to pry them open and flip out the meat, they could open as many as 750 oysters an hour. The oysters were then packed in iced wooden kegs ready for delivery to various markets.

The building was used in the oystering business until John Thomas's retirement in 1956. Donated to the Museum in 1970, it was brought from New Haven by barge, restored on land, and then placed on its waterfront pier by crane in 1984.

Oyster Farming

As demand for oysters grew and natural beds were overfished, oystermen in the 1850s learned to cultivate oysters in undersea "farms." Surveyed and buoyed, these private grounds extended along the Connecticut shore. Some were used for spawning new crops, often using adult "seed oysters" dredged from natural beds. Others were used for growing oysters to market size. Oystermen working on private grounds were free to use steam- or gasoline-powered vessels to dredge, and to haul their dredges with power. Like farmers tending their fields, oystermen laid down old shells, which they called "cultch," for juvenile oysters to settle on, then mopped up the predatory sea stars and otherwise protected their "crop" for the three years it took the oysters to grow to market size.

NEW HAVEN OYSTER TONGING SHARPIE

Perhaps derived from the long, narrow dugout canoes used by Native American and early Connecticut oystermen, the sharpie was developed around New Haven, Connecticut, about 1850. Sharpies were used by oyster tongers, who anchored their boat with a pole driven into the shallow oyster bed and then stood on the rail and used long-handled tongs to gather oysters from the bottom. A boat of this size could carry about 150 bushels of oysters. A centerboard helped these flat-bottom boats track straight as they sailed swiftly about the sheltered waters where they worked. This boat was built about 1890 and has been restored at the Museum.

NELLIE
OYSTER DREDGING SLOOP

Europeans introduced tongs and dredges to scrape up the oysters, establishing the technology for a flourishing fishery. Launched at Smithtown, Long Island, New York, in 1891, the *Nellie* represents hundreds of sailing oyster boats used in New York and Connecticut waters. Her shallow, wide hull allowed her to lift and carry heavy loads on shallow oyster beds; a centerboard could be lowered to help her sail straight; and her simple sloop rig was easy to handle with a small crew of about three men.

The *Nellie* fished for oysters from Port Jefferson and Patchogue, Long Island, for 10 years. Then John Ryle bought her to dredge for oysters near Stamford, Connecticut. She was one of nearly 350 sailing craft licensed to work Connecticut's natural oyster beds in 1900. To protect the beds, Connecticut prohibited dredging under power on its natural beds from 1881 to 1969.

Natural beds were public property, but sea bottom without oysters could be bought (later leased) from a town or the state and held as private property. John Ryle owned 78 acres of bottom near Stamford. By 1914 Ryle had outfitted the *Nellie* with a gasoline engine. Perhaps the engine was originally used to get her out to the natural beds, where she had to work under sail, but later her sailing rig was removed. Then she would have worked as a dredge boat on Ryle's private oyster ground.

In the face of pollution, storm damage to oyster beds, and public health concerns about oysters, the Connecticut oyster industry contracted through most of the 1900s. After a long working career, the *Nellie* was donated to Mystic Seaport in 1964. She was partially rebuilt as a sloop soon after. A full restoration in 2000 returned the *Nellie* to the configuration she had before her engine was installed.

How Did the *Nellie* Fish?

When dredging, sloops like the *Nellie* let their sails luff (flutter) and used the tide to push them across the oyster beds, dragging as many as six dredges. At the end of the drift the oystermen pulled in the 80-pound dredges by hand, then sailed back to dredge again. After catching 100 or more bushels of oysters, the boats would either bring them in to the local oyster processors or deliver them to "buy boats" that sold them for seeding private oyster grounds.

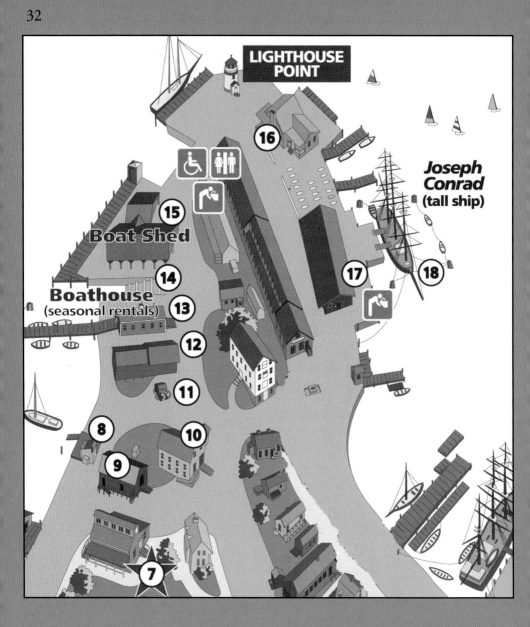

7. Mystic River Scale Model
8. Lobstering Exhibit
9. New Shoreham Life-Saving Station
10. John Gardner Boat Shop
11. Robie Ames Salmon Shack
12. *Australia*

13. Boathouse
14. Marine Railway
15. Tom Clagett Boat Shed
16. Youth Training Building
17. Catboat Exhibit
18. *Joseph Conrad*

7 MYSTIC RIVER SCALE MODEL

What did the Mystic River area look like in the mid-1800s? This spectacular model, over 50 feet long, is built to the scale of 3/32 inch=1 foot, or 1/128th scale. It provides Museum visitors with a dramatic bird's-eye view of history. After years of continuing research and construction, the model features more than 250 detailed dwellings, shops, barns, and lofts, as well as five local shipyards. At the Greenman Brothers' yard (on the current site of Mystic Seaport) the famous clipper *David Crockett* (built in 1853) is on the ways. Other vessels typical of those built in Mystic, from yachts to fishing sloops to steamboats, lie in the water or at dockside all along the river.

Sound-and-light shows help visitors understand what went on in the active communities of Mystic River (in the Town of Groton on the right) and Mystic Bridge (in the Town of Stonington on the left) during the height of shipbuilding, between about 1850 and 1880.

The scale model has been evolving since 1958. Some of the original volunteer model builders are still at work on it.

8 LOBSTERING EXHIBIT

Noank, Connecticut, three miles from here at the mouth of the Mystic River, was a major New England lobster port in the 1800s. Between 1875 and 1900, her 40 lobstermen set their traps across a 60-mile stretch of water from Montauk, Long Island, to

Martha's Vineyard, Massachusetts. The lobster shack was the lobsterman's shoreside base of operations, where he made or repaired his traps, painted and rigged the distinctive buoys that floated above his traps to identify them, and stored his gear.

Many Noank lobstermen used seaworthy Noank sloops for setting and hauling their traps. During the height of the season in August and September, the fleet often landed 500 lobsters a day, kept alive in wet wells built into the sloops. Many lobstermen had floating wooden pens called "cars" in which they stored up to 600 lobsters before sending them to market in New London and New York, often aboard smacks like the Museum's *Emma C. Berry*. Noank lobstermen switched to powered lobster boats around 1910. A few lobstermen still operate out of Noank today, but all of the original Noank lobster shacks were destroyed in the 1938 hurricane.

Based on lobster shacks in photographs of Noank, this building was constructed in 1981 to house gear typical of the late 1800s. Inside, it is set up for steam-bending and building the typical round-top traps out of oak lath and ribs cut by local sawmills. Reproductions of a lobster car and a lobsterman's "Noank sharpie" rowing skiff are stored outside.

35

9 NEW SHOREHAM LIFE-SAVING STATION

The most dangerous part of a ship's passage is often its approach to shore, where safe harbors are separated by long stretches of beach or bluff, and ledges and shoals wait to snare ships. During storms, with wind blowing onto these lee shores and rain or snow making it very difficult to navigate, shipwrecks were common on all coasts of the U.S. Although Massachusetts had a Humane Society to rescue victims of shipwreck as early as 1784, and the federal government began funding lifesaving stations in 1848, it was not until 1871 that Congress enacted legislation establishing a formal lifesaving service, which became the U.S. Life-Saving Service in 1878. It was incorporated into the U.S. Coast Guard in 1915.

Constructed at Old Harbor on Block Island, Rhode Island, in 1874, the New Shoreham Life-Saving Station is one of the last survivors of the many Atlantic seaboard stations built to government specifications from Maine to Florida. Nicholas Ball, a Block Islander and U.S. Congressman, was instrumental in having it built, and he became its first keeper. A station like this was manned during the stormier months, from about September to May, by a keeper and six surfmen. The ground floor contains the boatroom and the messroom. The surfmen slept in a bunkroom upstairs (because of the narrow stairway it is not accessible). The surfmen kept a constant vigil for ships in distress, from the roof platform and by patrolling the beach, especially at night and during storms. Weekly, the crews practiced their lifesaving drills, launching their surfboat off the beach and using a Lyle gun and breeches buoy apparatus to haul people ashore from a stranded vessel.

The crew of this station was involved in several rescues from stranded ships during the 16 years the station was in service. Before the turn of the century it was auctioned off, moved several hundred feet, and used as a stable and blacksmith shop. In 1967 it was

U.S. Life-Saving Service Halfway House

At night, and sometimes during the day, surfmen of the U.S. Life-Saving Service walked the beach to warn off ships standing into danger and to report stranded or wrecked ships so rescue efforts could begin. The halfway house was the place where men on the beach patrol exchanged brass tags with a patrolman from the adjoining station to indicate that their patrols had been completed.

Formerly located half-way between the Cahoon's Hollow and Pamet River Life-Saving Stations on Cape Cod, the small building was typical of halfway houses, which were used by the U.S. Life-Saving Service and Coast Guard from the 1870s through the 1930s. Unused for several years, and half buried in the sand in a nearly inaccessible area, the house was extracted by helicopter, trucked to Mystic Seaport in 1969, and restored during 1974.

purchased by the Block Island Club and moved two miles overland to Great Salt Pond, for use as a clubhouse. In 1968 it was brought to Mystic Seaport by barge in exchange for a reproduction.

The station was restored and formally dedicated in 1975. Unlike most stations, it faces inland, as it did in Old Harbor—so that the large doors open onto the town roads for moving the boat or beach cart. The boatroom has original gear for the two most common methods of rescue, the breeches buoy and the surfboat. The metal lifecar could be used in place of the breeches buoy in especially violent seas. During the warmer months, the Museum's Special Demonstration Squad performs the breeches buoy rescue drill on the village green so visitors can understand the work of the U.S. Life-Saving Service.

10 JOHN GARDNER BOAT SHOP

This shop is named for the late John Gardner, who was renowned for reviving interest in traditional wooden boats. He taught here from 1970 to 1995. The purpose of the Boat Shop is to study, teach, and encourage the construction and use of traditional small sailing and rowing boats. This is accomplished through research into small craft construction, publication of articles and books, sale of lines plans and construction drawings, and teaching of boatbuilding classes at Mystic Seaport.

The annual Small Craft Workshop, a weekend gathering of traditional boat owners, professional and amateur boatbuilders, and small-boat enthusiasts, allows participants to compare boats and ideas and to learn more about wooden boat construction and use. Small Craft Weekend is scheduled for the first weekend in June each year.

The building was originally a workshop located along the river just south of the Museum's Preservation Shipyard. It was moved to this site in 1958.

11 ROBIE AMES SALMON SHACK

In many areas of the U.S., fish that spend most of their lives in the ocean return to the rivers of their birth to spawn. Like Native Americans before them, European fishermen learned to catch these passing fish during their seasonal migrations. For several months the fishermen would be busy catching and processing their fish and maintaining their fishing gear. When the migration ended the fishermen packed up their gear until the following year and pursued their other occupations, especially farming or day laboring. Among the fish pursued in this way was the Atlantic salmon, which spawned in most northeastern rivers until industrial dams increasingly blocked its migration.

In 1837 Isaac Ames bought property alongside Penobscot Bay in Lincolnville, Maine, and started a salmon-fishing business as a sideline to farming. In 1838 or 1839, he built this small shack, which was used during the off-season to house the mooring lines, nets, floats, and buoys that made up his "hook of nets." During the spring salmon run up the Penobscot River, he set his pound net alongshore to entrap salmon swimming up the bay. This floating maze of netting fished night and day while members of the Ames family did their farm chores. Once or twice a day they would row out in their round-bowed salmon wherry to the "heart" or inner room of their net and kneel in the bow of the boat to remove the fish. Isaac's son George Ames continued the business, as did his grandson Robie Ames, who fished until 1947. By then, salmon had become so scarce that he carefully stored all the gear in the shack and locked the door.

In 1967 Mystic Seaport was able to purchase all of his fishing equipment, and soon Robie donated the shack to the Museum. After partial disassembly, the building was moved to the Museum in 1969. The restoration was completed in 1977, and today the building is fitted out with the original salmon fishing gear that came from the family.

12 *AUSTRALIA* COASTING SCHOONER

Sailing vessels carried freight along the coasts of North America from colonial times until World War II. The centerboard schooner *Australia* was built as the *Ella Alida* in 1862 at Great South Bay, Long Island, New York. She was sold to British interests, renamed *Alma*, and taken to Nassau in the Bahamas for use as a blockade-runner during the Civil War. With the Southern states fighting for independence, and in need of manufactured goods from Europe, President Abraham Lincoln had imposed a naval blockade to starve the South into submission. But some British and Southern merchants made a lucrative business of running munitions and goods through the blockade, returning with valuable cotton. While attempt-

The *Australia* under sail in 1935. (Mystic Seaport 1997.14)

ing to run a cargo of rum, salt, and guns in to the small port of Darien, Georgia, the *Alma* ran aground and was captured by a U.S. Navy warship.

The little schooner was then sold at auction, renamed *Australia*, and became a coaster in Chesapeake Bay. For more than 60 years she sailed the Bay as a typical small coasting schooner, carrying everything from shellfish to grain and produce. At some point her hull was lengthened 10 feet.

The 70-foot, two-masted vessel spent her last years in Chesapeake Bay as a yacht for the duPont family. The family donated her to Mystic Seaport in 1951 for use as a sail education vessel. For 10 years she was used as a dormitory in the Museum's sail training program. In 1961 she was hauled out for restoration, but the decay was too extensive to make rebuilding worthwhile. The Museum decided to preserve the *Australia* as an exhibit of ship construction. Today you can walk through and around this beached vessel, examining her "bones" as you might examine a skeleton.

Australia Beach

On the beach in front of the Ames Fish House, Museum educators help visitors learn about the marine environment during the warmer months. Among the specimens that can be seen are some of the "blue immigrants"—species that have hitched rides on the bottom of ships, or more recently in ballast water carried by large cargo ships. Local examples are the Green Crab, introduced in the 1700s, the European Common Periwinkle, introduced in the 1840s, Dead Man's Fingers (Codium) introduced in 1957, and the Asian Shore Crab, introduced in 1988. With few natural predators, these species have sometimes overpopulated, changing the balance of species in their new environments.

13 BOATHOUSE

By the late 1800s, many seaports had a maritime equivalent of a livery stable, where boats could be rented for pleasure or business. To give visitors a chance to try different traditional wooden watercraft types and to see Mystic Seaport from the water, the Museum operates the Boathouse boat livery during the warmer months. Visitors may rent a variety of rowing and sailing craft by the hour.

14 MARINE RAILWAY

Shipyards specializing in ship repair have used marine railways since the early 1800s. This small marine railway, named Firefly, was built in 1957, when this site was the Museum's shipyard. It is still used for hauling smaller vessels for maintenance. When the vessel is positioned in its cradle on the submerged rails, the winch in the small shed hauls the cradle up the rails.

The adjoining White Boatshop is used for boatbuilding classes taught by Museum staff. A list of classes can be found on the Museum's Web site. The *Brilliant* Shop is used for storage and preparation of equipment for the Museum's sail-training schooner, *Brilliant*.

BRILLIANT
SCHOONER YACHT

The *Brilliant* is a 61-foot auxiliary schooner used to introduce young people to the arts of seamanship aboard a traditional vessel. Designed by the firm of Sparkman & Stephens and constructed in 1932 by the City Island, New York, shipyard of Henry B. Nevins, the *Brilliant* is one of the finest wooden boats of her size ever built in the United States. The schooner has participated in several Bermuda Races and crossed the Atlantic in 1933, sailing from the Nantucket light-ship to Bishop's Rock Light off England in the record time of 15 days, one hour, 23 minutes. During World War II she served with the Coast Guard on the antisubmarine "picket patrol." In 1946, she was restored as a yacht by the well-known sportsman Briggs S. Cunningham, who gave her to the Museum in 1952 for training purposes. Since then, she has taken more than 7,500 participants to sea. In 2000 the *Brilliant* again crossed the Atlantic, winning the Tall Ships 2000 Race, then toured European ports before returning by way of the Azores and the Caribbean.

When in port, the *Brilliant* lies here at Scott's Wharf, named in honor of avid Mystic Seaport members Robert and Ellen Bird Scott. Visitors may be disappointed to find her wharf empty, but the *Brilliant* spends many of her days at sea when an adult or teen program is in session.

15 TOM CLAGETT BOAT SHED

This simple structure is named for an enthusiastic Mystic Seaport member, volunteer, and donor. In winter it is used for storage of some of the boats used in the Museum's Boathouse program. In the warmer

months it is used for outdoor dining and special programs.

Next to the boat shed is Bartram Dock, named for J. Burr Bartram, a trustee of the Museum from 1939 to 1975. Large visiting yachts often tie up here in summer.

BRANT POINT LIGHTHOUSE

On the southwest point of the Museum grounds stands a copy of the lighthouse at Brant Point on Nantucket. When the first Brant Point Lighthouse was built in 1746, it was the second lighthouse in the colonies (the first being Boston Light, dating from 1716). The wooden tower on which this one was modeled, built in 1900, is the lowest lighthouse in New England, with its light only 26 feet above sea level. Like the original on Nantucket, which has a 1,300 candlepower electric light and is visible for ten miles, the Brant Point Lighthouse copy contains a fourth-order Fresnel lens. The Museum's lighthouse was built in 1966.

The lighthouse has been a significant device for identifying harbors and warning sailors of coastal dangers since ancient Egyptian times. Lighthouses have gone through a long evolutionary process, beginning with burning piles of wood, then using whale oil lamps for illumination, and culminating in the present automated, electronic lighthouses. Developed in France during the 1830s, the Fresnel lens, which efficiently focuses light to create a strong beam, was one of the most significant improvements in lighthouse technology.

16 YOUTH TRAINING BUILDING

Mystic Seaport offers sailing and maritime skills classes to both young people and adults as part of its mission to educate about the historic influences of the sea on American life. The Mariner Training Program was established on the *Joseph Conrad* as a summer camp for sea scouts in 1949. The program expanded to include an at-sea component in 1953 with the arrival of the schooner yacht *Brilliant*. To serve as a base and classroom space for the sailing

programs, the Theodora Griffis Latouche Youth Training Building was dedicated in 1961. It continues to serve the *Joseph Conrad* Summer Camp Program for boys and girls aged 10 to 15, the community sailing program, and other educational programs. Students learn to sail in nine-foot Dyer Dhows, a recreational version of a boat originally designed as a navy lifeboat during World War II. In summer, you may see them sailing in the river, with their colorful sails marked to indicate which yacht club donated each boat. Information on the sailing programs can be found at the Museum's Web site, www.mysticseaport.org

17 CATBOAT EXHIBIT

Popular for both work and play in the shallow waters of southern New England, Long Island, and New Jersey, the catboat was developed before 1850. Its characteristic feature is a single mast set at the very bow, with one large sail. Catboats usually have wide, shallow hulls as well, often with a centerboard to help them sail straight in spite of their shallow draft.

Selected from the many examples in the Museum's watercraft collection, this exhibit shows the variety of traditional catboats. The 12-foot Beetle Cat is a pleasure boat first built at New Bedford, Massachusetts, in 1921 and still in production today. During the summer you can see Beetle Cats under sail, and even try one, at the Museum's Boathouse. *Sanshee* is a 14-foot Cape Cod-type catboat built at Wareham, Massachusetts, for pleasure use before 1925. Other cat-rigged pleasure craft are the 14-foot North Haven Dinghy, a type that has been raced in Maine since 1887, and the 13-foot Woods Hole Spritsail Boat, built for racing at Woods Hole on Cape Cod about 1914. Working catboats in the exhibit include the Newport shore boat, built for fishing and lobstering in Rhode Island around 1860, and the classic 20-foot Crosby catboat *Frances,* built at Osterville in 1900 and used for many years at Nantucket.

Also on display are three examples of the exceptional yacht design and construction of the Herreshoff Manufacturing Company of Bristol, Rhode Island. *Fiddler,* a Buzzards Bay 15 class racing sloop with typically long ends, was built about 1902 and owned by Caroline Dabney, who won the 1904 Beverly Yacht Club series with her all-female crew. Her family donated the boat to Mystic Seaport in 1959.

With her short ends, the 26-foot *Alerion III,* built in 1913, is a contrast to *Fiddler. Alerion* was a favorite of her famous designer, Nathanael Greene Herreshoff. He used this beautifully simple daysailer in Narragansett Bay and at Bermuda. *Alerion* was donated to Mystic Seaport in 1964.

Nettle, a Buzzards Bay 12 1/2-foot-class daysailer, is one of the popular class designed by Herreshoff in 1914. The fiberglass version called the Bullseye is still racing today. Catherine Adams received *Nettle* as a Christmas present from her father, Charles Francis Adams. Almost 50 years later, after she, her children, and her grandchildren had learned to sail in *Nettle,* she donated the boat to Mystic Seaport in 1963.

18 *JOSEPH CONRAD* SCHOOLSHIP

The veteran training ship *Joseph Conrad* sailed under three flags before mooring permanently at Mystic in 1947.

Built in Copenhagen in 1882 and named *Georg Stage* as a memorial to the young son of Frederik Stage, a prominent ship owner, the 111-foot, iron-hulled vessel was designed to

accommodate 80 boys in training for the Danish merchant service. From her launching until her sale in 1934, more than 4,000 cadets sailed in her for six-month training cruises in the Baltic and North seas. Run down by a British freighter in 1905, the *Georg Stage* sank, taking 22 young men with her. However, she was raised and repaired with watertight bulkheads and soon resumed her career.

Retired after 52 years, the vessel was about to be broken up when Captain Alan Villiers bought her in 1934. Under the British flag, and renamed the *Joseph Conrad*, she carried Villiers and his crew on a 58,000-mile voyage around the world that lasted more than two years. Once again boys were her crew: a nucleus of older teenagers from big four-masted barks, officers from the Cape Horn trade, eight American cadets and eight British, with a sprinkling of Australians and New Zealanders.

In 1936 George Huntington Hartford bought her, added a modern engine, and used her for three years as a private yacht. Under his ownership, the *Conrad* was matched against the yacht *Seven Seas* in a square-rigged ship race from the United States to Bermuda and back, each winning one leg. In 1939 the *Conrad* was transferred by Hartford to the U.S. Maritime Commission and continued in service as an American training ship until 1945. After a two-year lay-up she became, by act of Congress, the property of Mystic Seaport.

At Mystic Seaport the *Conrad* is an exhibit as well as a training ship for the Mystic Mariner Program, and at times serves as a dormitory for visiting groups taking part in the Museum's educational programs. Thus, although she goes to sea no longer, she continues to fulfill her original purpose.

The *Joseph Conrad*, ca. 1900. (Mystic Seaport 1962.1252)

MARITIME COMMUNITIES

The early colonial outposts planted in North America soon turned from defensive installations to small versions of the seaports in the mother countries across the Atlantic. Wharves reached out, warehouses sprang up, and merchants, craftsmen, and the full range of urban occupations settled in. Though originally seen as colonial suppliers of commodities to their mother country Great Britain, Boston, New York, Philadelphia, Charleston, Portsmouth, and Newport reached out to the world through sea trade to become cultural centers and the first American cities. By the time the colonies rebelled in the American Revolution, the seaport of Philadelphia was second only to London in its size and sophistication in the British Empire.

The seaports of the new United States remained the most vibrant centers of commerce and culture through the 1800s as the nation continued to export raw materials and import manufactured goods from around the world. The wharves and waterfront streets bustled with the flow of goods and people. From the 1820s to the 1920s, waves of immigrants flowed through American seaports, more than 35 million of them in search of opportunity, making those threshold cities even more diverse. Anything seemed possible in a seaport.

With territorial expansion, other ports grew into prominence: the Mississippi-Ohio River ports of New Orleans, St. Louis, Cincinnati, Pittsburgh, and other ports on the great river system of the heartland; the Great Lakes ports of Buffalo, Detroit, and Chicago; and the gold-rush port of San Francisco, and others on the West Coast. With its large harbor, expansive spirit, and commercial ties inland (especially via the Hudson River and Erie Canal), alongshore, and offshore, New York remained America's leading city and port into the mid-1900s. With more limited means, other seaports specialized. Salem, Massachusetts, had its greatest success in trade with Asia. Gloucester, Massachusetts, and Biloxi, Mississippi, specialized in fishing. Nantucket and New Bedford, Massachusetts, and New London, Connecticut, were the principal ports of the whaling industry. Others, like Mystic, Connecticut, specialized in shipbuilding.

As the threshold between land and sea, the seaport has been the most vibrant of American communities. Until the mid-1900s the sea was the only practical way to travel and exchange goods across oceans. But shipping and seaports have changed dramatically in the past 50 years. The revolutionary shift to containerized shipping moved maritime commerce away from traditional waterfronts.

For 300 years American seaports were great cities. The modern port is now the maritime equivalent of a parking lot, and traditional waterfronts are a place of contemplation, not commerce. We now travel by air, exchange information electronically, and think of the sea mostly in terms of recreation or defense. Yet, more than 75 percent of what we use each day still reaches us by sea, and—no matter how quiet their waterfronts—American seaports are still among our most important urban areas.

MARITIME COMMUNITIES AFLOAT

Like shoreside communities, shipboard communities differed in structure and composition depending on the trade and the time. At one extreme was the oceangoing merchant ship, with a crew ranging from 10 men in a small trader to 60 or more in a large vessel or clipper ship. In these communities of work, the population was divided into two shifts to work on a four-hour schedule around the clock. Only during the two-hour dog watches between 4:00 and 8:00 P.M. (used to swap the work schedule each day) and on Sunday did the crew have free time. As the owners' representative, the captain had ultimate authority and responsibility. The first and second mates served as the watch foremen, managing their half of the crew in response to the captain's orders. In each watch were several experienced sailors whose rating as able bodied seamen earned them a bit more than less-experienced ordinary seamen or inexperienced "boys" or greenhands were paid. Also aboard were several men less skilled as sailors than as tradesmen, such as a carpenter and sailmaker. Most important for health and morale was the cook, who turned the ship's preserved provisions into something edible. These shipboard communities were normally very temporary, dissolving at the end of each passage after surviving the rigors of work at sea.

A whaleship, such as the *Charles W. Morgan,* represented another approach to maritime labor, where the crew shared in the profit or loss of the vessel rather than receiving a wage. Whalemen normally signed aboard for the entire voyage, knowing it might last two years or longer. Their share of the profits was determined by the skill required in their job on board. A whaleship crew was further divided into six-man boat crews for the whale hunt and then restructured itself to process the whale.

The crew of a New England fishing schooner like the *L.A. Dunton* also worked on a share rather than a wage system. Sometimes the shares were apportioned based on individual skill, so the "high-line" fisherman who caught the most earned the most. By the time of the *Dunton,* however, most fishermen received equal shares of the profits. Like whalemen, fishermen were sailors, specialized hunters, and processors of the catch. More than any other form of seafaring, fishing often operated on a kinship basis.

Each of these shipboard communities under sail represented a diverse population incorporating a wide range of races and nationalities. Even in the time of slavery, black men could find a measure of equality in a ship's crew, and ships had to rely on whatever laborers could be enticed to share the hardships, dangers, and isolation of shipboard life, whether teenagers from New England or men from Europe, South America, or the Pacific islands. Each crew represented a balance of teamwork and individual initiative, a structure that required strangers to become the closest of associates for the good of the ship.

Engine-powered vessels gave rise to a different kind of maritime community. As steamships became reliable, with no need for auxiliary wind power, the sailors lost their main function and became primarily maintenance workers for the ship. Those who made the ship go worked below to serve the engines. The "black gang" of coal-heavers and firemen endured intense heat to keep the boilers fed with coal. Their supervisors, the engineers, kept steam flowing and the engines turning, as in a factory ashore. This population, which could number more than 100 on a large steamship, worked a rotating schedule like sailors, but it was a community apart, which had little contact with the deck crew of sailors and few strictly maritime skills.

Even though the skills of the small crews that operate the massive motor ships of today are far different from those of seafarers under sail, the world of the ship remains a unique mobile community, tying together the world's communities of commerce and culture by sea.

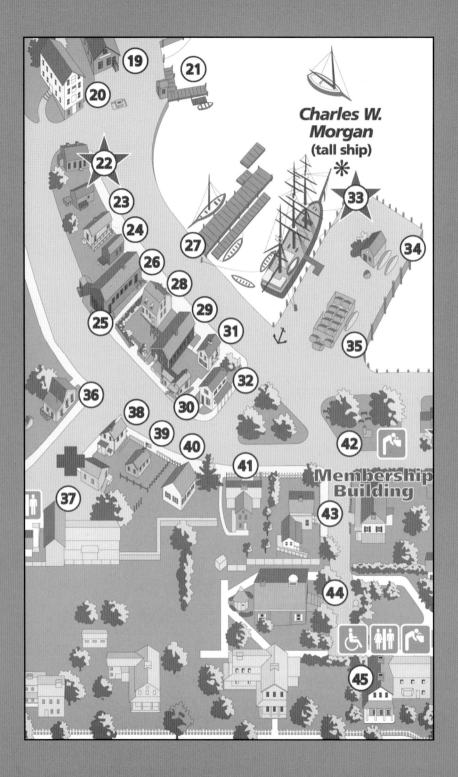

19 PLYMOUTH CORDAGE COMPANY ROPEWALK

The Plymouth Cordage Company was established on the outskirts of Plymouth, Massachusetts, in 1824 by Bourne Spooner, a Plymouth native who had learned the art of ropemaking in New Orleans. Because he was strongly opposed to slavery he established his own ropewalk back home with free labor rather than in New Orleans with slave labor.

For his ropewalk, Spooner chose a point of land with enough water to dock small vessels. A nearby millpond provided water power to operate the ropemaking machinery. The original ropewalk was 1,050 feet long (four times as long and twice as wide as the section preserved here). A walk of that length could produce finished rope in the mariner's standard length of 100 fathoms, or 600 feet.

Spooner ran the company until 1870. He was both a moral leader and a hands-on manager, like many successful New England industrialists of his period. In the community he was known as an ardent abolitionist and temperance man. Frugal in business, and hesitant to invest in new technology, he kept his company flexible, constantly seeking the best prices for raw materials, experimenting with new products, trying new markets in distant ports, and competing or collaborating with other ropemakers to retain a share of the market. Between the quality of its products and Spooner's personal efforts for 45 years, the Plymouth Cordage Company succeeded during rapidly changing times.

By the end of the 1800s ropemakers had invented machines to spin, twist, and coil rope in one compact operation, so they no longer needed a long ropewalk like this, except to produce large-size ropes and other special products. In 1951, Plymouth Cordage Company workers saved this 250-foot section of the original ropewalk building and reassembled it here with its machinery.

There are three main steps in the production of rope. Natural fibers are first spun into yarn, a process represented on the top floor of the ropewalk exhibit. Many yarns are twisted together by means of a moving "truck" on the ropewalk floor to form a strand. Then three (or more) strands are twisted together in the

opposite direction to form rope. The tension of twisting the parts in the opposite direction at each step is what holds rope together.

Early rope was made of either American or Russian hemp, but by the 1830s abaca (manila) was being imported from the Philippines and rapidly became the preferred fiber. Manila is cleaner than hemp, as well as more durable and flexible, and does not have to be tarred, as did hemp, to resist deterioration by heat, rain, and salt water.

Plymouth Cordage made rope for all kinds of vessels. It supplied most of the rigging for the *Great Republic*, the largest clipper ship ever built, and the manila running rigging for the influential schooner yacht *America* of 1851. One specialty was whale line, the strong, flexible line attached to harpoons used by whaleships like the *Charles W. Morgan*. Ironically, Plymouth cordage was also used in oil-well drilling, and cowboys favored Plymouth cordage for their lariats.

Although the ropewalk is set up as if to function, the machinery is not powered.

20 CHARLES MALLORY SAIL LOFT

Charles Mallory came to Mystic in 1816, having just completed his apprenticeship to a sailmaker in New London. He prospered as whaling and shipbuilding grew in the village, and by the 1860s he was one of the state's most successful shipowners. He had already moved into maritime finance

each of whom supplied his own tools and bench.

Sailmakers used canvas of different weights, which came in bolts about two feet wide. After the canvas was cut to the pattern on the floor, it was sewn together with heavy waxed thread as the sailmaker sat on his bench with the canvas across his knees. A sailmaker's palm served as a thimble to push the heavy, triangular needle through the canvas. To finish the sail, a bolt rope was stitched around the edges to reinforce the sail, and fittings for attaching the sail to the yard or mast were added.

As a display of early sewing machines indicates, stitching the pieces of cloth together could be done by machine as early as the 1860s, but adding the bolt rope and fittings continues to be handwork on canvas sails even today. Maintenance work on the Museum's sails and the building of new sails for our exhibit vessels still take place in this sail loft.

by the time this building was built, about 1839, but his firm, Mallory & Grant, and other sailmakers continued to use the loft into the 1870s. Originally located downriver from where the Museum now stands, the building was brought here by barge in 1951.

Beginning in the 1870s, blueprints that included the sail dimensions were supplied by a ship's designer. Prior to that time (and frequently even after that date), sailmakers made their own plans and patterns. After measuring the masts and yards of the ship, the sailmaker drew a plan and then outlined each sail on the floor of the loft. In order to have as much uninterrupted working space as possible, even the stove was suspended from the ceiling. A loft like this might employ three or four men,

20 RIGGING LOFT

The work of the rigger was another essential shipbuilding trade in the age of sail. All of the lines and ropes on a vessel—both for supporting the masts and for raising and operating the sails—were installed by the rigger.

Working from plans or dimensions supplied by the designer, the riggers worked in the loft while the ship was being built. There they made

up the miles of standing (permanent) and running (movable) rigging required. Until 1850 natural fibers—hemp and manila—were used to make the rope of various types and sizes. After that date, wire rope and chain were increasingly used, especially for standing rigging, which required great strength and little stretch. As soon as the ship was launched, the rigger and his men went on board to step the masts and install the rigging.

Many of the tools in this exhibit were given to the Museum by Captain William J. White of New London, who in his lifetime rigged more than 350 vessels.

20 SHIP CHANDLERY

Although the term is derived from the French for a seller of candles and soap, a ship chandler carried almost everything that would be needed on board ship, from candles and clothing to food and hardware. The ship chandlery was a retail and wholesale source of supplies for both individual seamen and vessels. The chandler knew the needs of his local economy and was a specialist in providing goods needed for whaling, commercial shipping, fishing, or shipbuilding.

Contracting for provisions at the chandlery was the responsibility of the ship's agent, a man authorized by vessel owners to manage supplies and equipment, as well as repairs, freight, towage, and the hiring of officers and crew. A chandler himself might serve as an agent for ships.

Lack of shipboard refrigeration meant that food supplies on a sailing vessel were largely limited to salt fish, salt beef, salt pork, hardtack, molasses, potatoes, onions and other winter vegetables, spices, and flour. Rum and tobacco were also in stock at a chandlery. At a time when most clothing and footwear was made to order, sailors could buy readymade clothing and boots, as well as blankets, pipes, and knives at a chandlery. The chandler would supply the same kinds of goods to a ship for its slops chest, which contained necessities that could be sold to the sailors while at sea and deducted, with interest, from their pay. Supplies for the ship itself ranged from navigational instruments to lanterns, buoys, logbooks, and inkstands. Needles, beeswax, and canvas were available for use in repairs aboard ship as well as for the sailmaker in port. In addition, marine hardware, paints, oils, and compounds were available.

This representative ship chandlery displays a large number of objects from the Museum's collection. All sorts of items that would have been available in a chandlery of the 1800s are on view, from anchor balls and lights to bomb lance guns, mast hoops to brass fittings, and cordage to caulking irons.

21 DAVE'S CLAM SHACK

This small waterfront utility building was originally a woodshed attached to the house that is now the Children's Museum. It was moved to this site in 1953 as a snack bar. Now it is a workshop for the Museum's Special Demonstration Squad, which demonstrates maritime skills around the grounds in the warmer months.

22 JAMES DRIGGS SHIPSMITH SHOP

This shipsmith shop was built at the head of Merrill's Wharf (now Homer's Wharf) in New Bedford, Massachusetts, by James D. Driggs in 1885. It is the only manufactory of ironwork for the whaling industry known to have survived from the 1800s.

Driggs served his apprenticeship during the early 1840s (about the time the *Charles W. Morgan* was launched) with the James Durfee

Block Island Fire Engine #1

Fire has always been a hazard, especially in a densely populated seaport with its many industries and stocks of flammable cargoes. Mystic had several serious shipyard and downtown fires in the mid-1800s, which resulted in the formation of volunteer fire companies. In a shipbuilding community, the fire engine might also be put to use "watering" new vessels to swell their seams before they were launched.

Block Island Fire Engine #1 was built by Gleason & Bailey in the 1850s and operated by volunteer firemen to protect the wooden homes, businesses, and hotels of that island community. The pump-break mechanism on the engine could develop enough pressure to throw a stream of water 100 feet. Pulled by hand, this pumper would be accompanied by a hose cart with two 500-foot hoses.

Company, then the largest and most productive blacksmithing business in New Bedford. He and another Durfee employee, Joseph Dean, established their own shop near Merrill's Wharf in 1846, under the name of Dean & Driggs. The two smiths produced high-quality whalecraft—harpoons, cutting irons, ship's fittings, etc.—in a successful partnership that lasted almost 30 years. Their shop, located in an alley that came to be known as Driggs Lane, was equipped with five forges and machinery run by power tapped from a neighboring flour mill. They employed as many as three journeymen at a time, one

of whom was Lewis Temple Jr., son of the African American shipsmith who in 1848 invented the practical toggle harpoon that made capturing whales much more successful.

In 1885, with the whaling industry on the wane, and having himself reached the age of 65, Driggs relocated to this new, smaller shop that he built with his grandson's help on the wharf. This shop served Driggs's needs until 1902, when he sold it to Ambrose J. Peters. Driggs died shortly thereafter.

Peters had served his apprenticeship in the machine shops that served New Bedford's textile mills, and when he purchased this shop shipsmithing was not much in demand. He added a large ell to the rear of the shop (primarily for storage) and branched out into the lubberly pursuits of general blacksmithing. After his death in 1918, his brother, Charles E. Peters, operated the business until 1924—three years after the *Charles W. Morgan* was retired. Although they were not the specialists that Driggs had been, the Peters brothers continued in whalecraft manufacture when only a handful of whaleships, including the *Charles W. Morgan*, were left in service. Merrill's Wharf was the last outpost of Yankee whaling, and C.E. Peters was probably the last whalecraft manufacturer in America.

Charles Peters's widow sold the shop in 1925, and it was placed on display at Round Hill, the estate of Colonel E.H.R. Green in South Dartmouth, Massachusetts, where the *Charles W. Morgan* was also exhibited. In 1944 the shop was brought to Mystic Seaport to rejoin the *Morgan*. Mystic Seaport smiths operate the shop almost daily to demonstrate shipsmithing techniques and to produce ironwork for the Museum's vessels, including the *Charles W. Morgan*.

23 NAUTICAL INSTRUMENT SHOP

A seaport large enough to have captains and mates arriving and embarking almost daily would very likely have a business like our Nautical Instruments Shop. Here, the ships' officers could purchase or have adjustments made to their delicate and precise navigational tools.

To find their way at sea far from the sight of land, captains depended upon their quadrants and sextants—used to measure the angles between stars and planets, or between the horizon and a star (frequently the sun)—and their ultra-precise timepieces—marine chronometers—along with nautical charts and tables to determine their exact location on the watery world.

A person skilled enough to adjust a delicate chronometer could also repair the family mantelpiece clock. Opened in 1982, this exhibit includes many examples of both types of timepieces, along with tall case clocks, compasses, barometers, quadrants, sextants, telescopes, and charts from the 1800s. More information on their use is offered in the Museum's Planetarium.

24 GEORGE WASHINGTON SMITH MAST HOOP MANUFACTURER

On fore-and-aft-rigged sailing vessels, the forward edge (luff) of the principal sails is attached to the mast with wooden hoops that slide as the sail is raised and lowered.

Hoop-making reached its peak as the fore-and-aft sailing rig proliferated in the mid-1800s, and flourished until World War II.

The equipment in this building was used by the Smith family in Canterbury, Connecticut, well into

Hercules Model EK7 Engine

This simple single-cylinder (one-lung) engine with a flywheel is typical of many thousands found all over rural America after their introduction in the 1890s. They powered small shops, farm equipment, and lumber mills in the days before rural electrification and modern lightweight engines. These early gasoline and kerosene engines revolutionized a way of life dependant on animal power, water power, or steam power.

About 1900, George Washington Smith disconnected the water-powered turbine that drove his woodworking equipment and replaced it with a 6-horsepower Excelsior engine made by the Consolidated Engine Company of New York City. Like most of the hundreds of engine builders active in the early

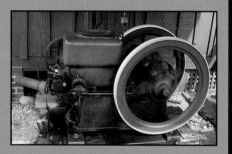

1900s, the Consolidated Engine Company lasted for only a few years.

This similar, 7-horsepower engine was built by the Hercules Company of Evansville, Indiana, which began production in 1912 and continued into the 1930s. By 1914 the company was building 150 engines a day, from 1 1/2 to 10 horsepower. This engine, built in 1917, was designed to run on either gasoline or cheaper kerosene. After Mystic Seaport acquired it in 1985, it was rebuilt and is often run as a demonstration.

the 1930s. Besides mast hoops, the Smiths also produced wagons, wheels, clothespins, washboards, stable forks, and belaying pins. During the growing season, this work was generally put aside in order to devote time to their orchard.

The shop is arranged as a small manufactory, with belt-driven machinery powered by overhead shafting. While a water-powered turbine or a small steam engine would have driven such equipment through the 1800s, the shop is set up as it might have been after 1900, with a one-cylinder engine to drive the shafting. The engine is demonstrated frequently during the year.

25 SHIPCARVER'S SHOP

Decorative shipcarving goes back to antiquity, and the craft was well developed for both warships and commercial vessels by the 1700s. By the mid-1800s ship decoration was less ornate, but sailing vessels continued to carry figureheads, or at least simple scroll billetheads, at their bows into the 1900s. Carvings on a vessel were meant to show pride and to capture the public's attention, just as carvings such as the Indians seen in front of cigar stores were used to advertise commercial enterprises on land. Figureheads commonly depicted the individual for whom a ship was named, or otherwise represented the spirit of its name.

Shipcarvers were normally independent craftsmen rather than shipyard employees. In Mystic, at a time in the second half of the 1800s when there were six shipyards in operation, the firm of James Campbell and John Colby did the carving for most of those shipyards. They also produced carvings for homes, made ornate fencing, and, in one case, carved a statue of Justice for a courthouse. The two men were involved with the local baseball club,

and the figurehead they carved for the ship *Frolic* was a woman holding a bat and ball.

Our Shipcarver exhibit represents the shop of an independent tradesman. The staff who work in the exhibit carve name boards, trailboards, figureheads, and sternboards for boats, as well as shop signs, tobacconists' figures, and decorations meant for the home.

Part of Mystic Seaport's large collection of figureheads is on display in the Wendell Building (#47). Look closely at the vessels along the waterfront to see other examples of shipcarving.

26 MYSTIC PRESS PRINTING OFFICE

At a time when news traveled fastest by ship, seaports were centers of information and among the first American communities to support newspapers and printers. The print-er, working at typecase and press, became a vital force in the economic, intellectual, and spiritual development of the nation. Due to its small size, Mystic did not have a newspaper until the weekly, four-page *Mystic Pioneer* was founded in 1859 and operated until 1870. It was replaced by the *Mystic Press* in 1873. Like most papers of the day, they carried many advertisements, along with local and political news, legal notices, letters to the editor, and often fiction. Like other seaport newspapers, they included a marine column listing arrivals and departures of ships.

Assembled to represent a newspaper and job printing shop of the later 1800s, the Mystic Press Printing Office contains the tools and technology of the journeyman printer's trade. From shops like this, with their Wells and Washington presses, platen job presses, and Cranston cylinder press, came the almanacs, newspapers, books, business forms, and handbills so important to the business, political, and social life of the community.

The building was constructed in 1952 as a memorial to Mystic busi-

nessman Andrew C. Colgrove. The printing office exhibit was set up in 1962.

27 MIDDLE WHARF

Middle Wharf is an example of a wooden pier, which was easy to build, but far less durable than a stone struc-ture like nearby Chubb's Wharf. A pier like this is subject to the effects of the same wood-consuming creatures that deteriorate wooden vessels, as a display panel on the wharf makes clear. Wood-eating gribbles eat away wood around the waterline, giving an hourglass shape to the pilings. Now that the Mystic River is so clean, boring ship-worms (actually related to clams) bur-

REGINA M. SARDINE CARRIER

The herring is one of those prolific fish that spawn on the northeast coast. But New England fishermen largely ignored herring until European canned sardines became popular in the U.S. in the 1860s. With canning already well established in the lobster, oyster, and vegetable industries, canners turned to herring to produce sar-dines. This industry flourished in the bays of far-eastern Maine from

the 1870s until the 1950s. The herring were corralled in net traps or brush fences called weirs, then bailed into boats for the trip to the cannery, where women and children sliced them and packed them in tin cans.

From the shores of Passamaquoddy Bay, the body of water separating eastern Maine from western New Brunswick, Canada, boatyards launched hundreds of small craft for the sardine industry. The *Regina M.*, built about 1900, illustrates one of several different types of sardine carriers used in the Passamaquoddy and Fundy Bays to collect herring from the fish weirs and transport them to the canneries around Eastport and Lubec.

The double-ended *Regina M.* was originally rigged as a sloop. However, as the internal combustion engine grew in popularity, many sardine carriers were fitted with engines to combat the fierce tides found in Passamaquoddy Bay. By 1909, the *Regina M.*'s equipment included a "Fairbanks Motor Co." engine that drove her at seven miles per hour.

In 1940, the Museum added the *Regina M.* to its collection of watercraft. However, before her arrival in Mystic, confusion regarding her true identity resulted in the conversion of her rig and hull shape to resemble a "pinky" (double-ended, two-masted schooner). Using new research, in 1992-94 Mystic Seaport restored her to the way she looked between 1909 and 1924.

row into our ships and pilings, gradually destroying them.

As another panel suggests, Middle Wharf is a good place to observe the birds of the Mystic River. Some, including the mallard, double-crested cormorant, herring gull, and osprey, are native to the area and are an important part of the larger marine environment. Others—including the rock dove (pigeon), introduced in the 1600s; house sparrow, introduced in the 1850s; starling, introduced in the 1890s; and mute swan, also introduced in the 1890s—were carried across the ocean as immigrants and have flourished in their new environment, sometimes displacing native species.

The vessels described below are often moored at Middle Wharf.

BRECK MARSHALL
CAPE COD CATBOAT

This reproduction of a Cape Cod catboat was built in the Museum's Small Boat Shop in 1987, using the techniques developed by the Crosby family of boatbuilders at Osterville on Cape Cod. The 20-foot boat is typical of those built for fishing and for pleasure use around 1900. At Mystic Seaport, the *Breck Marshall* is used in the warmer months to carry sight-seeing passengers on the Mystic River, sailing either from Middle Wharf or from the Boathouse. She

was built with funds donated by the Catboat Association and named for the late president of Marshall Marine, a catboat builder and enthusiast.

ARAMINTA
KETCH YACHT

In the warmer months, when she is not sailing, the graceful ketch *Araminta* lies on a mooring off the Museum waterfront. Designed in 1948 by L. Francis Herreshoff, the creative son of yacht designer Nathanael G. Herreshoff, the boat was built at the Hodgdon yard in East Boothbay, Maine, in 1954. The 33-foot boat was intended for daysailing in Maine waters, and her ketch rig, with the smaller sail aft (in contrast to a schooner like the *L.A. Dunton* or *Brilliant*), made her quite maneuverable and easy to handle. Since joining the Mystic Seaport fleet, the boat has been available for day charters with a licensed captain. Arrangements can be made by contacting the Boathouse (#13) or calling 860.572.0711, ext. 4233 or 5094.

Jane Burrows's Day

It's the 1870s. Do you hear the clatter of the sewing machine, the rumble of horses and wagons leaving Brown's livery across the way? Can you feel the breeze off the river and smell that blueberry pie baking? But what's that other odor—the horses or Mr. Burrows's pipe?

Welcome to the home of storekeeper Seth Winthrop Burrows and his milliner wife Jane. Look around. There is laundry to iron, the grandchildren's toys to pick up, weeds to pull, and an unanswered letter from a son at sea. For Mrs. Burrows, who is trying to run a household and contribute to the family's stretched finances, the work is never done. Sound familiar?

Mystic in the 1870s is a well-established, hard-working coastal community bustling with civic, church, and social activities. But a national recession and steady decline in wooden shipbuilding has hit local families and businesses hard.

What should Mrs. Burrows write to her stepson Ambrose, who is at sea? He will want news of his teenage sister Mabel, and word of the big fire at Mr. Cottrell's mill across the river. Perhaps she will share her worries about the recent outbreak of scarlet fever in the town. But should she trouble him with Mr. Burrows's business difficulties, or his disputes with the Temperance Committee over liquor sales that have led to her husband's latest court appearances?

28 BURROWS HOUSE

Details of its structure and architecture suggest that this house was built between 1805 and 1825. Originally situated on the opposite side of the Mystic River, the house was dismantled in 1953 to make way for a bank and was reassembled at Mystic Seaport. In the 1860s and early 1870s this was the home of Seth and Jane Burrows. By that time the house had been raised with an extra story beneath in which Seth sold groceries. He was notorious for selling liquor in a largely dry town. Jane opened a millinery business in 1874, and the exhibit is set up to represent her occupation as a dressmaker.

29 COOPERAGE

The cooperage manufactured round wooden containers, which we generally call barrels but are properly termed casks. These casks were an essential element both at sea and ashore, where wooden containers made from staves and hoops served many storage purposes. Aboard ship they held provisions, various kinds of cargo,

and, on certain fishing and whaling vessels, the catch.

Casks intended for spirits, molasses, whale oil, or other liquids had to be watertight, and the cooper who made these types of containers was a "tight cooper." Tight casks were usually made with hardwood—normally oak—staves and heads, with wooden or iron bands. Slack casks were used for flour, potatoes, apples, crockery, and just about any nonliquid goods that might have to be shipped from one location to another. These containers were made from softwoods.

Working with hand tools, the cooper split wood of the proper length to produce rough staves, then tapered their ends and beveled their edges with an ax, hollowed the inner surface with a draw knife, and cut grooves in both ends of the staves for the heads with a special plane. Tight casks were usually

When Is a Barrel not a Barrel?

When it's a hogshead or a tun. That's why the proper term is cask. A barrel for wine or whale oil is a cask holding 31 1/2 gallons. A barrel of petroleum, however, holds 42 gallons. Larger than a barrel, a hogshead typically holds 63 gallons, but by some measures can hold up to 140 gallons. The largest cask that was practical to transport was the tun, which held approximately 252 gallons (weighing approximately 2,000 pounds, or a ton). But of course all of these containers were built by eye, so each one had to be gauged with a special measuring rod to see how many gallons it really held.

charred on the inside to make the staves flexible as a series of smaller and small-er hoops was driven down to bend the staves into a finished cask. Often, pieces of reed, called flags, were placed between the staves to swell and caulk the cask to prevent leaks.

A cooper was a regular member of a whaleship's crew. He assembled pre-made casks— "shooks"—as they were needed to hold the valuable whale oil, and he was held responsible for leakage as well as accuracy of measure. Although whale oil was measured by the "barrel" of 31 1/2 gallons, a vessel like the *Charles W. Morgan* could hold hundreds of casks of various sizes, all packed on their sides with bung up. At the bottom of the hold, the ground tier of six-foot casks could hold hundreds of gallons each, while smaller casks of different sizes were stowed atop them.

The building in which the exhibit is housed was once a barn on the Thomas Greenman property. It has been modified to include typical features of a cooper-age: the bench at which the cooper shaped staves with axe and draw knives, a hearth large enough to work in while firing casks, a crane with a block and tack-le and chine hooks to hoist barrels, and a loft for storage.

30 H.R. & W. BRINGHURST DRUGSTORE AND DOCTOR'S OFFICE

Through the 1800s, the druggist was an important figure in any communi-

ty, but especially so in a seaport, where he supplied the medicines and medical supplies that were required by law to be carried on ships at sea. Few merchant ships carried a doctor, and the responsibility for treating the crew fell on the captain of the vessel, armed with a medicine chest and a manual describing symptoms and treatments. The seaport druggist did a substantial business stocking and refitting ships' medicine chests.

For home use, the druggist carried the popular drugs of the day and often sold spices, dyes, kerosene, and tobacco, as well as some groceries and household items. Two pharmaceutical collections are exhibited in this reproduced pharmacy interior of the period 1870-85. The Bringhurst collection was given to Mystic Seaport by Smith, Kline & French Laboratories, which had originally acquired it following the closing of the Bringhursts' Wilmington, Delaware, store. The Abram P. Karsh collection of pharmaceutical items came from the Philadelphia area. The exhibit was built by the Museum and opened in 1953.

A small doctor's office of the 1870-80 period adjoins the drugstore building. It is furnished with a massive Wooten desk, and rather gruesome-looking medical instruments that were the state of the physician's art in the mid-1800s. The doctor's office opened in 1962 and is dedicated to Dr. Alice Sheldon, who was lost at sea when the schoolship *Albatross* sank in a "white squall" in 1961.

Banknotes

Until the National Banking Act of 1862, the U.S. had no provision for a universally accepted paper currency. Gold, silver, and copper coinage of set value had been among the first priorities of the federal government, and the Spanish milled dollar—piece of eight—was legal tender in the U.S. until 1857. However, coins were never common enough to circulate throughout small-town America, and gold and silver were commonly hoarded during the economic depressions that beset the early nation. Small transactions with shopkeepers and between farmers and tradesmen were often recorded as book debts, with credit and debit accounts rectified periodically, and sometimes taken to court for resolution.

To make small transactions more efficient, local banks began to issue banknotes in the 1820s. These small-denomination notes were supposed to be underwritten by the bank's assets. To discourage counterfeiting, the notes were printed from copper plates engraved with increasingly intricate designs, produced by engraving companies such as the American Bank Note Company. Often they bore vignettes representing local scenes or themes of agriculture or commerce. Notes issued in maritime towns like Mystic often had images of ships, shipbuilding, or sailors. Locally, banknotes might circulate at face value, but if they traveled far from home, or if a bank's assets declined or the economy worsened, they were valued at a discount. Americans did not have a reliable circulating currency until the U.S. Treasury began issuing "greenbacks" during the Civil War and chartered national banks spread the federal system locally.

31 MYSTIC BANK

Businesses need money to grow. Mystic's shipbuilding and coasting trades were growing fast in the early 1800s, and soon a bank was needed in which to deposit profits and to borrow for expansion. In 1833, local businessmen opened the Mystic Bank in this small Greek Revival-style building at the head of the Mystic River, two miles north of here in Old Mystic.

The average Mystic family of 1850 would never have used the Mystic Bank. This was a commercial bank, where checking and savings accounts as we know them were not available. Dependable businessmen could secure loans and mortgages here, to support solid ventures like shipbuilding or farming. Though the Mystic Bank was founded through the investments of a number of "directors," the bank actually had only two employees, the president and the cashier.

Vaults like the one in this bank were not built of granite to prevent burglaries. The real fear of the day was fire, and the bank's vault was the most fireproof place in town. The bank held its reserves of gold, silver, and banknotes inside the vault, alongside strongboxes containing customers' most valuable legal documents and business records. In seaports like Mystic, local

shipowners kept a separate strongbox for each vessel, containing accounts, registry papers, logbooks, and ledgers. The box marked *Acushnet* is a reproduction of the one in the Museum's collections that contained the papers of the Fairhaven, Massachusetts, whaleship on which Herman Melville shipped out as an ordinary seaman in 1841—the voyage that inspired his masterpiece, *Moby-Dick*.

In 1856, the Mystic Bank moved into a new, larger brick building nearby. This building was used for other purposes for almost 100 years until, in 1951, it was dismantled, brought downriver from its original site, and rebuilt here. The portico was replaced with an exact reproduction, a new floor was installed, and the walls were replastered.

SAMUEL THOMPSON'S NEPHEW & COMPANY SHIPPING OFFICE

The office of a shipping merchant is represented on the second floor of the Mystic Bank. In the larger seaports, some merchants specialized in operating ships. They owned or chartered (rented) the vessels they operated, which either ran on a regular route between ports or else "tramped" around the oceans, carrying whatever cargo was available to wherever it had to go. Sometimes they purchased cargoes to ship, hoping to make a profit on their sale in another port. Otherwise, they sold space in their ships and collected freight money from the shippers based on the weight or volume of each owner's part of the cargo. As immigration increased, some merchants specialized in shipping passengers.

At New York in 1818, former British merchant Jeremiah Thompson pioneered the concept of the sailing packet, which was guaranteed to sail on schedule rather than waiting until its hold was full. Offering predictable service, his Black Ball Line revolutionized transatlantic trade, and many packet lines were established. Reliable steamships began to compete with the sailing packets in the 1840s, but the Black Ball Line remained in operation until 1876.

This exhibit represents the firm operated by Jeremiah Thompson's relative Samuel Thompson, in partnership with John W. Mason. From their office on Duane Street in New York, they imported and exported all sorts of goods, but through the 1850s much of their business was in passengers. Each of their large, fine ships could carry several hundred immigrants in basic conditions. These immigrants usually traveled safely and in good health, but when the firm's new ship *Caleb Grimshaw* burned in 1849, more than 100 passengers were lost.

The contents of this exhibit were donated in 1966 by Wendell P. Colton Jr., in memory of Anne Mason Colton. The large, two-sided partners' desk made efficient use of space. The desk

organizer in the corner held the records of the firm's different vessels, while the letter press in another corner was used to make copies of business correspondence by pressing the letters to leave an ink impression on tissue paper.

32 SCHAEFER'S SPOUTER TAVERN

Seaport taverns were temporary homes to an ever-changing population of sailors who spent a few days of freedom ashore before shipping for another voyage.

Seaport taverns varied in size and refinement. More elegant establishments, such as the coffee houses of the early 1800s and fine hotels of the later years, catered to the influential members of the community like ships' captains, merchants, and politicians. These inns often served as the seat of local business and politics.

Lower on the scale were the cheap dives or grog shops in the waterfront district sometimes referred to as "sailortown." Often attached to sailors' boardinghouses, they saw many a shoreside spree during which "Jack Tar" might well be bilked out of his money by crimps, boardinghouse masters, prostitutes, and other "landsharks." Destitute, sailors then had little choice but to return to sea. Advocates of temperance and sailors' welfare tried to reform sailortowns, but after the deprivations of sea life it was hard to keep sailors away from the "pleasures" offered there.

Named for the fictional tavern in Melville's *Moby-Dick*, Schaefer's Spouter Tavern was built by the Museum in 1956 with support from the Schaefer family. The woodwork in the barroom is based on the woodwork of the Central House Inne in Stoddard, New Hampshire, built in 1833.

The adjacent gameroom is furnished with chairs and tables for the playing of

"The Spouter-Inn" (Herman Melville, *Moby-Dick* (1851), chapter 3)

Entering that gable-ended Spouter-Inn, you found yourself in a wide, low, straggling entry with old-fashioned wainscots, reminding one of the bulwarks of some condemned old craft. On one side hung a very large oil painting so thoroughly besmoked, and every way defaced, that in the unequal crosslights by which you viewed it, it was only by diligent study and a series of systematic visits to it, and careful inquiry of the neighbors, that you could any way arrive at an understanding of its purpose.

The opposite wall of this entry was hung all over with a heathenish array of monstrous clubs and spears. Some were thickly set with glittering teeth resembling ivory saws; others were tufted with knots of human hair; and one was sickle-shaped, with a vast handle sweeping round like the segment made in the new-mown grass by a long-armed mower. You shuddered as you gazed, and wondered what monstrous cannibal and savage could ever have gone a death-harvesting with such a hacking, horrifying implement. Mixed with these were rusty old whaling lances and harpoons all broken and deformed. Some were storied weapons. With this once long lance, now wildly elbowed, fifty years ago did Nathan Swain kill fifteen whales between a sunrise and a sunset. And that harpoon—so like a corkscrew now—was flung in Javan seas, and run away with by a whale, years afterwards slain off the Cape of Blanco.

Crossing this dusky entry, and on through yon low-arched way—cut through what in old

cards, chess, checkers, and dominoes. Nautical touches in both rooms characterize this as a waterfront tavern, a popular spot for seamen to gather. Light meals are often served in the barroom, and sea music is sometimes performed in the gameroom.

times must have been a great central chimney with fireplaces all round—you enter the public room. A still duskier place is this, with such low ponderous beams above, and such old wrinkled planks beneath, that you would almost fancy you trod some old craft's cockpits, especially of such a howling night, when this corner-anchored old ark rocked so furiously. On one side stood a long, low, shelf-like table covered with cracked glass cases, filled with dusty rarities gathered from this wide world's remotest nooks. Projecting from the further angle of the room stands a dark-looking den—the bar—a rude attempt at a right whale's head. Be that how it may, there stands the vast arched bone of the whale's jaw, so wide, a coach might almost drive beneath it. Within are shabby shelves, ranged round with old decanters, bottles, flasks; and in those jaws of swift destruction, like another cursed Jonah (by which name indeed they called him), bustles a little withered old man, who, for their money, dearly sells the sailors deliriums and death….

I sat down on an old wooden settle, carved all over like a bench on the Battery. At one end a ruminating tar was still further adorning it with his jack-knife, stooping over and diligently working away at the space between his legs. He was trying his hand at a ship under full sail, but he didn't make much headway, I thought.

At last some four or five of us were summoned to our meal in an adjoining room. It was cold as Iceland—no fire at all—the landlord said he couldn't afford it. Nothing but two dismal tallow candles, each in a winding sheet. We were fain to button up our monkey jackets, and hold to our lips cups of scalding tea with our half frozen fingers. But the fare was of the most substantial kind—not only meat and potatoes, but dumplings; good heavens! dumplings for supper! One young fellow in a green box coat, addressed himself to these dumplings in a most direful manner….

A tramping of sea boots was heard in the entry: the door was flung open, and in rolled a wild set of mariners enough. Enveloped in their shaggy watch coats, and with their heads muffled in woolen comforters, all bedarned and ragged, and their beards stiff with icicles, they seemed an eruption of bears from Labrador. They had just landed from their boat, and this was the first house they entered. No wonder, then, that they made a straight wake for the whale's mouth—the bar—when the wrinkled little old Jonah, there officiating, soon poured them out brimmers all round.

33 CHARLES W. MORGAN WHALESHIP

Of all the exhibits at Mystic Seaport, the most treasured is the 113-foot wooden whaleship *Charles W. Morgan*. Built in 1841 at the shipyard of Jethro and Zachariah Hillman in New Bedford, Massachusetts, and named for her first owner, she has out-lived all others of her kind.

During her 80 years of service the *Morgan* made 37 whaling voyages, ranging across the Atlantic, Pacific, and Indian Oceans in search of sperm and right whales. It took three to five years to take the approximately 50 whales required to fill her hold with oil. To be closer to the whaling grounds, the *Morgan* left her home port of New Bedford in 1886 and sailed out of San Francisco, making one-year voyages around the Pacific until 1903. She then returned to make a few more voyages out of New Bedford as the whaling industry came to an end.

Retired in 1921, the *Morgan* was featured in several movies before being preserved by Whaling Enshrined, Inc., and exhibited at Colonel Edward H.R. Green's estate at Round Hill in South Dartmouth, Massachusetts. Damaged by the 1938 hurricane, and without prospects for preservation, she came to Mystic Seaport in November 1941.

At Mystic Seaport, the *Morgan* has been given a new lease on life; however, her future vitality depends on continual preservation. A major program of restoration and preservation was begun in 1968 to repair her structural-

ly. From 1941 to 1973 she was exhibited here in a bed of sand. In January 1974 she was hauled out on the new lift dock in the Henry B. duPont Preservation Shipyard. Her hull proved to be in remarkably good condition, with much original wood remaining. As part of this work she was restored with the double-topsail bark rig she carried from the early 1880s through the end of her whaling career. During further restorations in the 1980s, she was largely rebuilt from the waterline up and is now accurately configured as she was around 1900. An additional restoration of her lower hull is planned.

A whaleship like the *Morgan* was a mother ship for three to five whale-boats, from which the whales were harpooned and then killed. Whaleboats are usually hanging in the *Morgan's* davits. For a closer view, visit the whaleboat exhibit on Chubb's Wharf or, in warmer months, watch the Special Demonstration Squad operate a whaleboat in the river.

On board the *Morgan*, look up. The mainmast stands 110 feet above the deck. Near the top of the foremast you can see the hoops used by the look-

The *Charles W. Morgan* at sea, ca. 1918 (Mystic Seaport 1978.207)

outs on watch for whales.

Amidships is the gangway, cutting stage, and hoisting tackle with blubber hook used to peel the insulating blubber from the carcass of a whale as it lay in the water alongside. On deck forward is the brick tryworks, where the oil was rendered out of the blubber. Aft, the small deck cabin under the skids for spare boats represents the one

added for the wife of Captain Tinkham in the 1870s. In the hurricane house at the stern are the galley (kitchen), storage areas, and the ship's wheel. In this simple, "shin-kicker" design, the wheel is mounted directly on the tiller that moves the rudder, so the helmsman must sidle when he turns the wheel. To hold a steady course he would study the compass mounted inside the cabin skylight and check the set of the sails. As a square-rigged ship, with sails suspended from yards perpendicular to the hull, the *Morgan* is especially well suited to sail with the steady ocean

winds blowing from behind.

Below decks aft is the captain's cabin and stateroom, which contains the gimballed captain's berth added for the wife of Captain Landers in the 1860s. At the foot of the companionway stairs are the pantry and messroom where the officers ate, and the cabins for the mates, boatsteerers (harpooners), and other specially skilled whalemen. The first mate kept the ship's logbook, making entries on the small desk in his stateroom. Amidships is the blubber room, where the crew worked on their knees to cut the large blanket pieces of blubber stripped from the whale into smaller pieces for the tryworks. Forward is the dark, cramped, often wet fo'c'sle (forecastle), which served as home for the common sailors "before the mast."

In the hold at the bottom of the ship, ballast, provisions and stores, and whale oil were packed in wooden casks of various sizes, overseen by the ship's cooper. The *Morgan* could carry about 2,500 "barrels"—31 1/2 gallons—of oil. In the hold you can see some of the *Morgan's* original structure. With one strake of the interior "ceiling" planking removed to promote circulation, some of her original frames are visible. We estimate that about 30 percent of the *Morgan* is original, but a major restoration in the near future will replace some deteriorated portions of that original structural timber.

The *Charles W. Morgan* was formally designated a National Historic Landmark by order of the Secretary of the Interior on July 21, 1967.

34 WHALEBOAT EXHIBIT

A fully equipped whaleboat is on display in the shed on Chubb's Wharf. The building, patterned after buildings on several of New Bedford's whaling wharves, was constructed in 1982. The whaleboat came to the Museum aboard the *Charles W. Morgan* in 1941. It is not known whether it was ever actually used, though it was likely built before 1920. The boat contains the gear typically carried in American whaleboats of the 1880s, and whaling tools are displayed above the boat.

The whaleboat was a beautiful craft adapted for a brutal purpose. You can see that this light, strong, double-ended boat was packed with gear for hunting the whale. Whaleships like the *Charles W. Morgan* carried between three and five whaleboats, hanging in davits ready for use. Each boat was

operated by one of the ship's officers and five oarsmen. About 1,200 feet of whale line were coiled in two tubs, then run around a loggerhead at the stern and forward over the oars to connect to the harpoons—which the whalemen called irons—at the bow. When the forward oarsman, usually called the boatsteerer, got the call, he stood, braced his leg in the "clumsy cleat" notch near the bow, and darted his irons into the whale. This anchored the boat to the whale. He then made his way aft to take the steering oar, and the officer came forward to kill the whale once it grew tired from pulling the boat in a "Nantucket sleighride" or diving—"sounding"—to escape. The officer used a long-shanked lance to pierce the whale's lungs and cause it to bleed to death. Once the whale rolled over, "fin out," in death, the boat towed the whale to the mother ship to be processed.

During the warmer months the Museum's Special Demonstration Squad rows a whaleboat to Middle Wharf to describe how whaleboats were used and demonstrate how maneuverable they were.

35 CHUBB'S WHARF

This wharf is modeled after the granite wharves at which the *Charles W. Morgan* lay in New Bedford, Massachusetts. The overall dimensions are 150 feet by 100 feet, which means that the *Morgan* or other large vessels can be moored along any of the three sides.

The funds to build this addition to the Museum's waterfront were given in memory of Hendon Chubb by his family. Mr. Chubb was a forceful leader of the insurance managing firm of Chubb and Son of New York. The wharf was built and dedicated in 1974.

In the center of the wharf is a representation of an oil pen, where casks of whale oil were stored before processing.

36 SEAMEN'S FRIEND SOCIETY READING ROOM

The American Seamen's Friend Society was established in the 1820s and incorporated in 1833 "to improve the social and moral condition of seamen." Growing out of the same religious revival that promoted temperance and the abolition of slavery, the society sought to uplift sailors by giving them an alternative to the bars, boardinghouses, and brothels that they commonly frequented while in port. The society established well-managed and reputable sailors' boardinghouses, including one for African Americans in New York. It encouraged sailors to save their earnings, which resulted in the founding of the Seamen's Bank for Savings. On shore, the society provided access to religious services, lectures, and

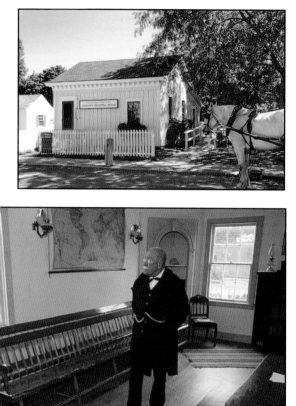

reading rooms. It was perhaps best known for the libraries of books that it placed aboard American ships for the use of sailors. Between 1859 and 1930 it sent out more than 13,000 of these seagoing libraries, each containing 40 books in a wooden case.

The American Seamen's Friend Society went out of existence in 1986, but its records are held by the G.W. Blunt White Library at Mystic Seaport, and this building serves as a testimonial to the good works of the society on behalf of sailors.

Often you will find one of the Museum's role players in this building, ready to talk to you about what it is like to live in an 1870s maritime community.

This building was originally a workshop on Clark Greenman's property and was located where the Museum's Planetarium is today. It was moved to its present site in 1960.

Music of the Sea and Shore

Music of the sea came in two forms: the work songs called chanteys, and leisure-time songs and instrumental pieces.

Chanteys take several forms. Capstan chanteys are long, evenly paced songs to ease the job of walking around a vertical winch called a capstan, which was used to raise the anchor. Capstan bars set into the capstan like spokes of a wheel gave the crew leverage to turn the capstan as they marched around it, often for an hour or more.

Halyard chanteys were used to coordinate the crew while raising sail. In this call-and-response style of song, the chanteyman sang a one-line verse as the crew rested, and the crew answered with a chorus that had two strong beats on which they pulled. For heavier hauling, a short-drag chantey had a one-beat chorus. Similar work songs were used by longshoremen loading heavy cargo and by fishermen handling heavy nets.

As the sea connected cultures, during the 1800s these songs developed to combine aspects of Irish and African musical traditions. "Chanteyman" was not an official position on board ship, but a sailor with a good voice and a quick wit was valuable in keeping the crew happy and efficient at its work. The chanteyman often improvised to make light of conditions, food, or other crew members, giving the sailors a little control over their situation.

Leisure-time songs and instrumental pieces were a mixture of popular songs and ballads of the day and improvised tunes made up on board. It was common for at least one sailor on board to have a banjo, concertina, fiddle, or other instrument, and to play during the two-hour, late-afternoon dog watch that served as the crew's daily leisure time.

Mystic Seaport has been a center for sea music performance since the early 1970s. The annual Sea Music Festival at the Museum in June brings together performers and participants from around the world. But you can hear sea music performed almost every day at Mystic Seaport. Depending on the season and the weather, scheduled performances are given at different locations around the grounds. Plan to sing along. And to see chanteys and other songs in action, in the warmer months. weather permitting, chanteys are used when the Special Demonstration Squad sets sails.

Often the Squad demonstrates the Dead Horse Ceremony, which was performed on some vessels to celebrate the end of the first month at sea. Since sailors were paid a one-month advance to settle their expenses ashore and outfit themselves before sailing (a sum that was frequently swindled from them), they did not begin to earn money until they had been at sea for a month. If the ship's captain agreed, they might amuse themselves by making a horse figure from canvas scraps and celebrate in a procession and song before hoisting the "dead horse" aloft and cutting it free to symbolize the end of their debt.

Special Demonstration Squad

Mystic Seaport preserves maritime skills as well as artifacts. Some of these traditional skills are demonstrated for visitors during the warmer months by the roving Special Demonstration Squad. You may find them aloft, setting square sails; on the water, describing and then demonstrating how a whaleboat was used; on the Village Green, performing the breeches buoy drill used by the U.S. Life-Saving Service; or elsewhere around the grounds. Check the daily schedule, and don't miss the chance to see maritime skills in action.

37 DISCOVERY BARN

The Discovery Barn is open seasonally and is designed especially for visitors aged eight and up. Parents and kids can explore interactive computer exhibits, furl a sail, or learn to tie sailors' knots. Visitors can also check out one of our many discovery boxes to learn more about the sea and sea life.

Attached to the Discovery Barn is the carriage shed from the Baptist Church in Winthrop, Connecticut, which was built before 1866 and moved to the Museum in 1954. It is currently used to house the draft horses used for carriage rides around the Museum grounds.

Village Green

Like a community's village green, this open space is used for activities, concerts, and simple recreation. The mast on the water side is used for a demonstration of the U.S. Life-Saving Service breeches buoy rescue drill in the warmer months.

The bandstand came from Fort Wright, a coastal artillery installation on Fishers Island, New York, just south of here. It was built in 1938 to replace the fort bandstand destroyed in the 1938 hurricane, and it was moved to the Museum in 1960. The Clift Block on the corner was moved to the site in 1956 and serves as office space.

38 GEORGE H. STONE GENERAL STORE

Built about 1850 as a house, this building was originally located in nearby Pawcatuck, Connecticut, and was given to the Museum in 1954. The creation of this exhibit was in large part the vision of George H. Stone, a retired merchant and resident of North Stonington, who personally stocked the shelves with his own collection of historic items. This exhibit was renovated recently with reference to the Greenmanville Store (which was established in 1863 in the building now called the Brustolon House near the Museum's main entrance). The store is filled with both original and reproduction items representing community life and foodways of the mid-1800.

39 BOARDMAN SCHOOL

Boardman School, named for the family whose land adjoined the school property, may have been built as early as 1765 in the town of Preston, Connecticut. When the North School Society of Preston split off to form the town of Griswold in 1815, Boardman School became Griswold's District Seven School, and the building served as a classroom for six generations of Connecticut children.

Boardman School is typical of the many rural district schools in New England during the 1800s. Pupils attending this school studied reading, writing, grammar, arithmetic, and geography. More advanced pupils might be taught algebra, Latin, or French.

By the middle of the 1800s, one-room schoolhouses like this one were coming under attack for being inefficient and outmoded. In 1882 this school was described as "A backward one, and the house poor. The blackboard is too small to be of much use." Another Connecticut town official commented: "Many of our school houses are in a miserable condition, possessing less attraction outwardly than our prisons while within they are dark, gloomy and comfortless. They are all destitute of an appearance of any outhouse." With educational reforms and introduction of the grade system, one-room schools became obsolete and had been retired by the early 1900s.

A number of the desks, the woodstove, and the blackboard came with the school when it was moved to Mystic Seaport in 1949.

Mildred C. Mallory Membership Building

A nonprofit membership organization from the very beginning, Mystic Seaport has grown from nine members in 1930 to more than 22,000 in 2005.

Begun in 1963, this building was opened in 1965 to benefit members of Mystic Seaport. The building houses the Museum's Membership Department and has a lounge where members may rest and have a cup of coffee or juice. The building incorporates the granite lower story of an early-1800s Mystic house ruined by the 1938 hurricane.

The Boardman School in its original location.

40 FISHTOWN CHAPEL

During a religious revival in the late 1800s, this rural chapel was constructed at Fishtown, a crossroads west of Mystic, for use by "Baptist, Methodist, Episcopal, Congregational and other evangelical denominations," according to its charter. Built by local subscription in 1889, it was used for occasional services by visiting ministers and for Sunday school. For about 12 years it was also used as a schoolhouse. Unused after 1925, the chapel was given to Mystic Seaport in 1949. Moved and reconditioned as a nondenominational chapel, it was dedicated in 1950.

The exhibit and audio program within reflect some of the social issues addressed by local evangelical denominations.

41 BUCKINGHAM-HALL HOUSE

Life in this coastal farmhouse was filled from dawn to dusk, season to season, with hard work, business transactions, and the voices of visiting friends and relatives. Originally built by the Buckingham family around 1760 in Saybrook, Connecticut, near the only ferry crossing at the mouth of the Connecticut

River, the house was purchased in 1833 by William Hall Jr., from the estate of Samuel Buckingham. Here, the family of New York import merchant William Hall Sr. made their home in the 1830s. From their windows the Halls witnessed farmers moving goods to market, coastal traders and steamboats as well as ocean trading vessels moving up and down the river, and travelers as they passed down the road to the ferry. Though access to the river made goods from New York readily available, most of the foods and the fabrics needed for daily life were produced on the farm.

When construction of a new highway bridge across the Connecticut River threatened this structure with demolition in 1951, Mystic Seaport agreed to preserve it. The house was shipped to its present location by barge. Though it was reconstructed and furnished as a colonial home at that time, a second major restoration and re-interpretation of the house was completed in 1994, with the Buckingham family moving out and the Hall family moving in. The kitchen ell with its huge hearth is still the site for daily open-hearth cooking demonstrations, and the kitchen garden in the back is the source for much of the fresh produce. Quilting and weaving are also practiced in the house, and this is the site of various domestic arts classes throughout the year.

42 PERFORMANCE STAGE

In summer, this informal performance area is used for popular and interactive plays, such as "A Tale of a Whaler," that answer questions about maritime history in a fun and engaging manner for all family members. Check to see what is being performed during your visit.

43 CHILDREN'S MUSEUM

The Children's Museum provides a hands-on environment for children and their parents to explore together. The exhibit is organized around the theme "It's a Sailor's Life for Me." Children seven and under can swab the deck, move cargo, cook in the galley, dress in sailors' garb, and try out sailors' bunks. The Children's Museum also has a toy and game area, and a saltwater aquari-

Find Your Way at Sea

One approach is dead reckoning, based on the direction and distance traveled through the water. Finding the direction is easy with the use of a compass. To measure speed and distance, sailors tossed overboard a piece of wood on a knotted line and timed it with a sand glass that measured either 14 or 28 seconds. The spacing between the knots was the same proportion of a nautical mile that 14 or 28 seconds is of an hour. The number of knots pulled overboard equated to nautical miles per hour, so a ship's speed is measured in "knots."

Celestial navigation measures the ship's position in relation to the sun, moon, stars, and planets. The navigator's primary tool is the sextant, a protractor that measures the angle from the horizon to a celestial object, or between celestial objects. If sailors know the angles for a few stars, they can use a series of mathematical calculations and reference to tables published in the *Nautical Almanac* to plot their latitude (distance north or south of the equator) quite accurately.

To determine longitude (the position east or west of the prime meridian that today runs through Greenwich, England) sailors need to know the precise time simultaneously at the ship and on the prime meridian. This was simplified when the chronometer, a clock that keeps accurate time at sea, was developed in the 1700s. The chronometer is set to Greenwich Mean Time. Using a sextant to measure the angle between the sun and the horizon at the ship, noting the ship's dead reckoning latitude, and finding the declination of the sun from the *Nautical Almanac*, the navigator can calculate the precise time at the ship. The difference between ship's time and Greenwich time yields the longitude.

um. During the summer season, check out our water table with its fleet of toy boats.

The Children's Museum is located in the Edmondson House, an 1850s Greek Revival cottage on its original site. The house was originally owned by textile worker John Edmondson, who was married to the sister of the three Greenman brothers.

44 PLANETARIUM

Knowledge of the sun, moon, stars and planets has long been essential to mariners and explorers traveling across trackless oceans and unmapped continents. At Mystic Seaport, the importance of astronomy in navigation is demonstrated daily under the 30-diameter dome in the Planetarium.

First opened in May 1960, this Planetarium has acquainted more than two million visitors with the wonders of the night sky and the seamen's secrets of navigation. The lobby of the Planetarium contains a permanent exhibit showing the basic tools and techniques of navigation in

the 1800s and 1900s, including a sextant that visitors can use to measure an angle. Overhead, the ceiling is decorated with an orrery, a mechanical model of the solar system. The sun should be at the center, but cannot be shown because of the greatly compressed distance scale used in the orrery. Made to the same scale as the planets, the sun would be over seven feet in diameter and Pluto would not even fit inside the room!

The projection equipment used for the live programs given in the Planetarium was designed and built for the Museum by the Spitz Laboratories. The dodecahedron (twelve-sided) figure in the center of the room projects about 700 stars that could be seen from the Northern Hemisphere. A second dodecahedron can project the stars of the Southern Hemisphere. As the sun, moon, and planets appear to move with respect to the stars, their images are projected by individual devices. Additional projectors show the earth from its center, various coordinate systems and shapes useful in teaching celestial navigation, recent images of planets, and other wonders of the universe. From time to time meteors or "shooting stars" whiz across the night sky.

The Planetarium also acts as the weather and emergency preparedness center for Mystic Seaport. Weather data and forecasts are compiled from weather stations atop build-

ings on the Museum grounds and from the Internet and shortwave radio stations. Daily weather forecasts, area weather readings, tide predictions, and astronomy notes are sent by email to anyone who wishes to receive them. Send your email request to

planetarium@mysticseaport.org. An Emergency Preparedness Manual has been compiled and revised annually during the past 35 years and has served as a model for many other museums and historic sites around the world.

Many school groups, scout groups, yacht clubs, religious groups and family groups come for special programs that support their curricula or unique interests. Evening courses in navigation, astronomy and weather are conducted, as are daytime workshops in sextant use and basic navigation. Summer evening programs and free community telescope viewing of the planets are also conducted. For more information go to our Web site, www.mysticseaport.org, or call 860-572-0711.

45 THOMAS GREENMAN HOUSE

The three stately Greek Revival-style houses preserved by Mystic Seaport are important reminders of the community once called Greenmanville. Built within four years of each other between 1839 and 1842, the houses represent the affluence and importance of the Greenman brothers, George, Clark and Thomas, who left Westerly, Rhode Island, for Mystic. Here, they made their fortunes as shipbuilders, manufacturers, and men of commerce (see page 88).

The first floor of the Thomas Greenman house, built in 1842, is open to Museum visitors, who can enter the double parlor on the south side of the house and see the large dining room and sewing nook on the north. Two of the rooms have been decorated and furnished in the manner of a prosperous Victorian home of the 1870s. A few pieces of the furniture are from the Greenman family.

Thomas Greenman's granddaughter, Mary Stillman Harkness, donated the house to the Museum in 1945, and the exhibit was opened in 1952. The kitchen wing and the upstairs rooms are used as Museum offices.

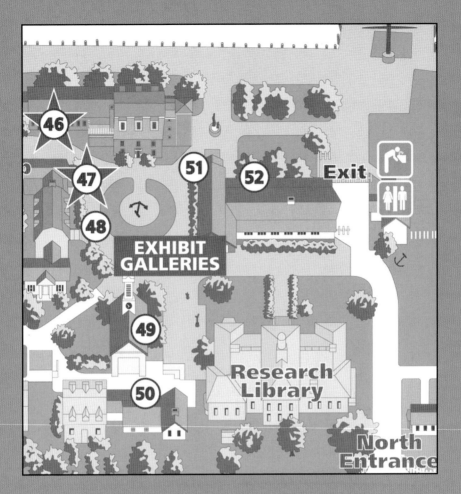

46. Voyages Exhibit
47. Figurehead Exhibit
48. Mallory Buildings
49. Greenmanville Church

50. Schaefer Exhibit Hall
51. *Benjamin F. Packard* Ship Cabin
52. North Boat Shed

46 STILLMAN BUILDING

The Stillman Building is the cornerstone of the Museum's gallery complex. Originally built in 1862 as an addition to the Greenmanville Manufacturing Company textile mill, the three-story waterfront structure became the Museum's primary exhibit building in 1939. It is named for one of the Seaport's founders, Dr. Charles K. Stillman.

Since 2000, the building has housed the Museum's signature exhibit, *Voyages: Stories of America and the Sea.* Here you can discover how your life is shaped by the sea in ways you may never have imagined. The exhibit fills all three floors of the Stillman Building (now serviced by an elevator) with art, artifacts, audio and video programs, and computer games illustrating how Americans have always been connected to the sea. The first floor looks at immigration, river and coastal trade, international trade, the U.S. Navy, recreational uses of the sea, and the breadth of involvement of the U.S. Coast Guard. Prominent artifacts include the refugee boat *Analuisa* which helped 20 Cubans cross the Straits of Florida to a new life in 1994; a girl's view of life on a trading ship of the 1880s; and a feature on 1990s U.S. Navy submariner Joe Mikolajczak and his family.

The second floor contains the section on sea resources gathered through whaling and fishing. Artifacts and films tell stories of whaling, codfishing, and fish and oyster processing, as well as the modern stories of a Native American fisherman of the Columbia River, a woman fishing in Alaska, menhaden fishermen in the

South, and a Stonington, Connecticut, fisherman. The third floor looks at the sea's influence on art and inspiration, with a prominent display of the whaleman's art of scrimshaw—engraving and carving whale ivory and bone. Visitors may create their own works of sea-inspired art in the Inspiration Station or participate in a program in the performance space.

47 FIGUREHEAD EXHIBIT

The Wendell Building houses some of the Museum's most dramatic figureheads and ships' carvings. The most romantic and mysterious of all artifacts from the age of sail, these figureheads, billetheads, and catheads also demonstrate the extraordinary skill of their craftsmen. Of particular interest are the eagle head from Donald McKay's magnificent ship *Great Republic*, the fierce figurehead from the Mystic-built ship *Seminole,* and the grand goddess from the yacht *Iolanda*, which can also be seen in small scale on a model of that huge steam yacht. For more information on figureheads, visit the Shipcarver's Shop.

Originally the machine shop of the Greenmanville Manufacturing Company textile mill, the Wendell Building was opened to the public as the first exhibit building at Mystic Seaport in 1934. In 1949 it was remodeled and dedicated to George Blunt Wendell, a clipper ship captain from Portsmouth, New Hampshire, whose collections are at Mystic Seaport.

CLIFFORD D. MALLORY JR. CIRCLE

Once the site of the Greenman brothers' wooden textile mill, this circle was created in the 1930s when the entire Museum was housed in the three brick buildings around it. The circle is dedicated to the memory of a lifelong friend and longtime trustee of the Museum.

The 7,000-pound anchor displayed in the circle was salvaged off Newport, Rhode Island. Its size and shape match British Admiralty specifications for a bower anchor of a 74-gun ship of the line during the American Revolution and War of 1812. It was probably lost by one of the British warships that blockaded Newport during the Revolutionary War. The wooden stock was reproduced at Mystic Seaport.

Carried on the bow as their name suggests, bower anchors were a ship's largest. By tradition the starboard (right) anchor was called the best bower. The port anchor was called the small bower even though it was usually the same size.

48 MALLORY BUILDINGS

The Mallory exhibit buildings commemorate five generations of the Mallorys engaged in maritime commerce. The first Charles Mallory, born in Waterford, Connecticut, in 1795, had just finished his apprenticeship as a sailmaker and was headed for Boston in 1816 when he stopped in Mystic, found work here, and decided to settle. He established a sail loft, prospered, and invested his profits in sealing and whaling ships. Eventually he became a prominent shipbuilder and shipowner. His son, Charles H. Mallory, went to sea and served as captain of several of his father's vessels. He, too, bought a shipyard on the banks of the Mystic River and became involved in an important coastal steamship line operating between New York and Texas. He was also a prominent sailor in the early years of

American yachting. C.H. Mallory's shipping and yachting interests were passed on to his son, Henry Rogers Mallory, and to his grandson, Clifford Day Mallory. Clifford D. Mallory was the president of Mystic Seaport from 1937 until his death in 1941. Upon his brother's death, Philip R. Mallory became president of the board of Mystic Seaport, and later Clifford D. Mallory Jr. served in that position. Clifford's son Charles is now a trustee of the Museum.

The C.D. Mallory Building was dedicated in 1948. The P.R. Mallory Wing was added in 1969 and serves as changing exhibit space. Downstairs is an exhibit on American yachting, featuring the yacht-turned-slaveship *Wanderer*, the prominent grand yachts of entrepreneur Arthur Curtiss James, and the expansion of yacht racing to everyday Americans, as represented by the International Star Class.

49 GREENMANVILLE CHURCH

During the heyday of Mystic's shipbuilding activity in the 1850s, and for a generation thereafter, the Greenmanville Seventh-day Baptist Church was the focus of the area's considerable Seventh-day Baptist community. Like other Baptists, they believed in voluntary baptism as an admission of faith; like Jews and a few other Christian sects they followed the Old Testament in worshiping on the seventh day—Saturday. Seventh-day Baptists involved themselves in the social issues of the day, supporting the temperance movement, opposing slavery, and promoting education and missionary efforts.

The Greenmanville congregation was an offshoot of the Greenman brothers' own home parish in Westerly, Rhode Island. After holding services in their homes or other halls, the growing congregation built the church about 1851 (the original site is adjacent to the present main entrance to Mystic Seaport) largely through the support of the Greenman and Fish shipbuilding families.

In accordance with Seventh-day Baptist custom, the Greenman shipyard and textile mill worked from Sunday through Friday. Worship services were held each Saturday, when most of the other Mystic shipyards were in full operation. At least once, the neighboring Mallory shipyard, run by Congregationalists who celebrated the Sabbath on Sunday, launched a ship on a Saturday while the Greenmanville Church service was in progress. A resident reminisced that the excitement of the event interrupted the pastor's sermon in mid-sentence, as the congregation turned for a better view of the launching ways, cheering in unison when the climactic moment came. The service then resumed, no doubt in some disarray.

With the decline of the shipyard during the 1870s and 1880s, the congregation was depleted and the church was finally closed in 1904. After use as a private residence and apartment building, the old church was acquired by Mystic Seaport in 1955.

Through the generosity of the Arthur Curtiss James Foundation, the Museum was able to move the building to its present site and restore it. The tower clock in the steeple was added after the church was acquired by the Museum. Built in 1857 by the Howard Clock Company of Waltham, Massachusetts, the clock is on permanent loan from Yale University, where it was located in the Old South Sheffield Hall of the Sheffield Scientific School. The elaborate clockwork may be seen inside the building.

G.W. BLUNT WHITE LIBRARY

Mystic Seaport's maritime library is among the most significant in the nation. A research library specializing in American maritime history, the holdings include 70,000 volumes of books and periodicals, 2,000 rolls of microfilm, 1,000 ships registers, 1,000,000 manuscript pieces, 1,200 logbooks, 600 audiotaped oral history interviews, 200 videotaped interviews, and 9,000 maps and charts. In addition to its physical holding, the Library also has an extensive digital collection. More information is available on the Museum's Website, www.mysticseaport.org.

Opened in 1965, the library was dedicated in memory of G.W. Blunt White, a well-known yachtsman and longtime Museum trustee. Besides stacks and a reading room, the Library contains the classroom used by the undergraduate Williams College-Mystic Seaport Maritime Studies Program and the summer graduate Munson Institute program.

50 R.J. SCHAEFER EXHIBIT HALL

The R.J. Schaefer Exhibit Hall is the Museum's special exhibition gallery. Dedicated on June 7, 1975, as a tribute to Rudolph J. Schaefer, the building is home to changing exhibitions of Mystic Seaport's collections of maritime art and artifacts, and to loan exhibitions from other museums and private collections. The lobby has a dramatic display

of ship models called *Maritime Miniatures: Models from the Collection.*

Outside the R.J. Schaefer Building is the Wimpfheimer Terrace of Sea Sculpture. It is named for local manufacturer Clarence A. Wimpfheimer. The bronze sculptures currently on view are "Boy Feeding Seagulls" by Charles Parks (1976) and "Touch me" by Katherine Tod Johnstone in memory of Eleanor Bartram Radley. Nearer the waterfront is the fountain and sculpture "Three Dolphins" by Dorothy Bostwick Campbell (1965) in memory of Elinor D. Johnston.

51 BENJAMIN F. PACKARD CABIN

This complete cabin restoration of the *Benjamin F. Packard* is unique; no "Down Easters" like the *Packard* have survived. The original 244-foot square-rigged sailing ship, more than twice the length of the *Charles W. Morgan*, was built in 1883 at the shipyard of Goss, Sawyer & Packard in Bath, Maine, and named for one of the builders. "Down Easters" of the late 1800s were built to carry cargoes around Cape Horn between America's Atlantic and Pacific ports. The "Down Easters" replaced the clipper ships as the economic demands called for less speed and more cargo-carrying capacity. During most of her 25 years in the Cape Horn trade she was owned by Arthur Sewall & Co. of Bath, the largest firm of Cape Horn merchants at the time, and worked out of New York (though her official port of registry was Bath). She commonly carried mixed cargoes of manufactured goods 13,000 miles around Cape Horn from New York to San Francisco, then California wheat to Europe, then European goods to New York before heading round the Horn again.

In 1908 she became a "salmon packer," carrying fisheries workers and equipment from Puget Sound up to the Alaskan fish canneries in the spring and returning in the fall with the workers and the canned fish. After the 1925 season she made one last passage from Puget Sound to New York as a lumber barge in tow through the Panama Canal and was retired in 1927. After efforts to preserve her as a museum failed, she came to rest as an amusement park attraction in Rye, New York, where she was badly damaged in the hurricane of 1938. Before she was scuttled, a variety of artifacts, including much of the after cabin paneling and interior furnishings, were removed and brought to the Museum, where they were stored for almost 40 years.

Set up in the 1970s, the exhibit includes much of the officers' living quarters from the stern of the ship. Visitors first enter the officers' mess cabin. The mates' staterooms would have been behind the doors in the mess cabin. Next aft is the captain's day cabin, with its rich goldleafed maple-veneer panels, marble and brass fixtures, and plush upholstery. Some

Down Easter captains brought their wives to sea, in which case this would have been a well-decorated living room. Fartherest aft is the captain's stateroom. The excellence of the various woods, the fine veneers and graceful carving, and the elaborate decorations testify to the overall magnificence of the ship.

The *Packard* exhibit is housed in one of the buildings of the textile mill established by the Greenman brothers in the mid-nineteenth century.

52 NORTH BOAT SHED

The North Boat Shed is one of the two exhibit halls where some of the more than 500 historic watercraft in the Museum's collection are displayed under cover. The current exhibition is called "Our Grandfather's Boats."

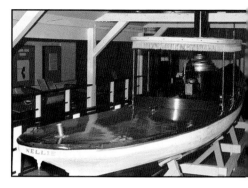

The small boats in this exhibit were built during the century from 1850 to 1950 and represent tremendous changes in the way Americans lived and went boating. In 1850, boats were built one at a time in small shops, for fishermen and others who worked for their living on the water. By 1950, small boats were being built by the hundreds in factories, and sold like automobiles to Americans who just wanted to get out on the water and have fun. In 1850, traditional small craft were either pushed by the wind or pulled along by the strength of the rower. By 1950, these types had been overtaken by wave after wave of

Greenmanville, ca. 1873. (Mystic Seaport 1972.92.513)

GREENMANVILLE

The maritime community of Greenmanville was an industrial village that manufactured ships. The site of Mystic Seaport was a mix of meadow and marsh along the Mystic River estuary when George, Clark, and Thomas Greenman bought the property in 1837. The three brothers had served their shipbuilding apprenticeships under their father in nearby Westerly, Rhode Island, in the 1820s. As local demand for small fishing and trading vessels increased, they joined their older brother Silas as journeymen at his shipyard near the head of the Mystic River, about two miles upstream from here. After Silas returned to Westerly in 1834 to establish a yard there, George continued to work as an itinerant builder locally while Clark and Thomas traveled to South America in 1836, aboard a vessel commanded by Captain Joseph W. Spencer, to build a river steamer for Mystic entrepreneur Silas E. Burrows.

When they returned, the three brothers established their own shipyard in 1837, purchasing 12 acres of land at the bend of the Mystic River, land with enough slope to launch a vessel and with clear access to deep water. Like the majority of American shipbuilders, the Greenmans began their yard by supplying the local need for vessels. The depression following the Panic of 1837 may have limited their options,

high-tech motor boats, powered by steam, naphtha, and then gasoline. Every boat in this exhibit has its unique history and its own stories to tell, stories about other times and other places and about people like our grandfathers.

Of special interest are a progression of powerboats: the elegant 1872 steam launch *Nellie*; the naphtha launch *Lillian Russell*, which used volatile naphtha instead of steam to power its engine; and the Thompson outboard runabout of the 1950s. Sailing craft include the sailing canoe *Patsy Green* in which Henry Wise Wood and his wife made a 900-mile ocean passage; the trophy-winning International Star Class racing yacht *Ace*; and the 25-foot sloop *Vireo*, bought by Franklin D. Roosevelt in 1920 and used by the Roosevelt family at Campobello Island. FDR sailed in the *Vireo* the day before he was stricken with polio in 1921.

yet their output was entirely typical of the many small shipyards whose scale and volume of work was determined by their local maritime economy. In Mystic, that was fishing and coastal shipping.

If it were not for their personal drive and fortunate circumstances, the Greenmans–like some of their contemporaries downriver in Noank–might have remained small local businessmen whose success would have depended on the local economy. But in the early 1840s they were able to enter a larger market. Thomas's and Clark's association with Captain Spencer during their expedition to South America paid off five years later when Spencer encouraged his employers, E.D. Hurlbut & Co. of New York (formerly, like Spencer, from the Connecticut River valley) to commission the Greenmans to build a large ocean trading ship. Then other New York shipping agents offered shipbuilding commissions, and in 1851 the Greenmans launched the large ship *Caroline Tucker* for New York merchant John A. McGaw, establishing a relationship that would last for almost 20 years. They continued to produce small fishing and coasting vessels for the local market as well. The very early screw-propelled steamboat *Florida* of 1844 suggests their willingness to be innovative.

With the success of their shipyard in the 1840s, a small community began to grow around it. The brothers built their own homes and rental properties, and others built homes and boardinghouses nearby. The community grew even larger when the brothers expanded into New England's thriving textile industry and built a woolen mill in 1849. They also operated farms that supplied some of the meat and produce consumed in the community.

As in many New England manufacturing villages established by one family, the Greenmans were both employers and community leaders. In business, the three brothers combined their skills. George was the businessman, Clark supervised the shipyard, and Thomas was actively engaged in the design of the ships and the details of their construction. The brothers' three houses, similar in design and standing side-by-side along the main road, suggest the unity of their mission. They also served the town of Stonington, in which Greenmanville is located, in various official positions.

The Greenman brothers brought something else to their community: a specific faith and the social issues it espoused. As devout Seventh-day Baptists, who observed the Sabbath on Saturday, the Greenmans differed from their Protestant neighbors in Mystic, but they attracted a number of shipbuilding and mill-working friends and relations of the same sect, and in 1851 they opened their own Seventh Day Baptist church. In their faith they were committed to the abolition of slavery, to temperance, and to missionary work.

As America neared the height of its maritime enterprise under sail, other shipyards flourished in Mystic as well.

The trade in China tea had influenced the development of fast sailing ships through the 1840s, but 1850 marked the beginning of the rush to clipper ship construction in reaction to the California gold rush. Locally, Charles Mallory, a prosperous sailmaker who had become a ship owner and shipbuilder, brought clipper construction to Mystic, launching the first one at his shipyard next to the Greenman yard in 1851. The Greenmans entered the field with the *David Crockett* in 1853. At 215 feet long, she was the largest vessel built by the Greenmans. Like the rest of the Greenman-built clippers, she was a "medium clipper," with a squarer hull in section than the more V-shaped hull section of the extreme clippers. By combining cargo capacity with good speed, the medium clippers extended the clipper era beyond the initial two or three years when extreme clippers could earn a profit rushing goods 13,000 miles around Cape Horn to San Francisco. With their long, sleek hulls and clouds of canvas sails, clipper ships are often considered the epitome of American naval architecture under sail, and the Greenmans built five of the approximately 400 vessels that qualify as clippers.

By the late 1850s, the glut of American ships, combined with the economic Panic of 1857, changed the picture for the Greenmans. Their best New York client remained, but they turned increasingly to steamboat construction as coastal steamboat connections increased. And, as recreation spread onto the sea, they built their first yacht.

Many of the Greenman ships had been used in the cotton trade, carrying America's primary commodity, produced by slave labor in the South, to the textile mills of New England and Europe. It was one of the ironies of American history that Northern abolitionists profited from and even encouraged slavery through this maritime relationship. A second irony occurred

The 162-foot bark *Coldstream* ready for launch at the Greenman shipyard, 1866. (Mystic Seaport 1939.2257)

after the Southern states seceded to form the Confederate States of America and President Abraham Lincoln mobilized the nation for a war of reunion. Although American maritime commerce was decimated by the war, and ships of the kind the Greenmans had built were dispersed to other nations, shipbuilders like the Greenmans actually prospered from the Civil War. With the government offering lucrative charter rates for steamers to carry troops and supplies south during the war, production increased dramatically. The Greenmans launched six large steamers in 1862, five in 1863, and four in 1864, some of them as much as 200 feet long. This was by far the busiest period in the Greenman shipyard.

The end of the Civil War brought an immediate drop in orders for ships.

With little support in Congress to subsidize the rebuilding of the U.S. fleet, the shipbuilding industry moved to where it could operate most economically. In New England this meant Maine. The Greenmans built a few more large sailing ships as well as a couple of the 15 gunboats constructed in Mystic for the Spanish government to quell a revolt in Cuba in 1869. However, as they reached their 60s the Greenman brothers became less active, even as the nation entered a decade of economic depression through the 1870s. The Greenman yard launched its last vessel in 1878, three years after the neighboring Mallory yard shut down.

With the end of shipbuilding, Greenmanville focused on textile production at the Greenman mill, then called the Mystic Manufacturing Company. By 1900, with the addition of the Rossie Velvet Company, it had become a bustling mill village with a decided German and French-Canadian flavor and no evidence of the shipbuilding industry that had brought it into existence. But like shipbuilding before it, the textile industry migrated, moving south in the mid-1900s.

Now, busier than ever before, Greenmanville's new product is maritime education. Since its establishment in 1929, Mystic Seaport has grown to become the nation's leading maritime museum. Each year, hundreds of thousands of visitors pass through Mystic Seaport, learning about America's sea heritage at the site where great ships were once built.

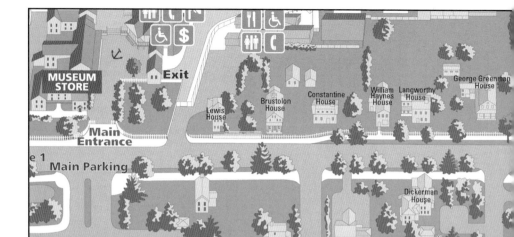

THE VIEW FROM THE STREET

THOMAS GREENMAN HOUSE

This house was built in 1842 for Thomas S. Greenman (1810-1887), the youngest of the three brothers who founded the George Greenman & Co. Shipyard. It was built in the Greek Revival style then prevalent in the U.S. The cast-iron fence was put up about 1866, and the porch and ornate decorations were added to the house in the 1870s.

CLARK GREENMAN HOUSE

This house was built in 1841 for Clark Greenman (1808-1877), the second oldest of the three brothers who founded the George Greenman & Co. Shipyard. It was built in the Greek Revival style then prevalent in the U.S. The cast-iron fence was put up about 1866, and the porch and ornate decorations were added to the house in the 1870s. The Clark Greenman House was further altered in the 1900s, but it is now painted to match its color scheme in the 1870s. It was acquired by the Museum in 1949 and served as the library before conversion to its present use as the Museum's administration building.

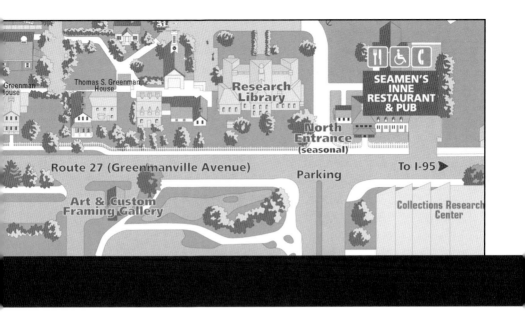

GEORGE GREENMAN HOUSE

This house was built in 1839 for George Greenman (1805-1891), the

oldest of the three brothers who founded the George Greenman & Co. Shipyard. The three brothers lived here until Clark and Thomas built their houses in 1841 and 1842. It was built in the Greek Revival style then prevalent in the U.S. The cast-iron fence was put up about 1866, and the porch and ornate decorations were added to the house in the 1870s. In style and paint color, the house now looks the way it did around 1900. The Museum purchased the house from George Greenman's great-granddaughter in 1970. The George Greenman House will eventually be restored as an exhibit building.

LANGWORTHY HOUSE

Part of this house was standing when brothers George, Clark, and Thomas Greenman purchased the

surrounding land in 1837 and founded the George Greenman & Co. Shipyard. They lived here until George Greenman built his house next door in 1839. About 1849 the 1 1/2-story house on this site was raised up and a new first floor and a two-story ell were added. For nearly 50 years it then served as a boarding-house for ship carpenters and other laborers, run by ship joiner David Langworthy (1818-1902) and his wife Fanny. The Langworthy House will be restored as an exhibit building.

WILLIAM HAYNES HOUSE

This house was built in the early 1850s by William Haynes (1820-

1905), a ship carpenter who often worked at the George Greenman & Co. Shipyard. The small room on the left side is a later addition, and the bay window was added in the mid-1900s when the building was used as a gift shop. It was acquired by the Museum in 1997 and is used for offices.

CONSTANTINE HOUSE

We believe this house was built in the 1840s, as Greenmanville expanded. George Greenman & Co. rented its two apartments to employees of the company's shipyard and textile mill. In the 1850s and 1860s it was occupied by the widow of a mill employee and the minister of the Greenmanville Seventh-Day Baptist Church. The dormer was added in the 1900s. Named for the family that last owned it, the Constantine House is used as an office building by Mystic Seaport.

BRUSTOLON HOUSE

This building was built about 1863 as the George Greenman & Co. store. The store, which sold produce and other goods to the shipyard and mill employees and nearby families until the 1880s, was located on the first floor, with living quarters for the storekeeper above. It later became an apartment house. Like many older American buildings, it was covered with ceramic siding in the mid-1900s. It was acquired by the Museum in 1994 and is used for offices.

LEWIS HOUSE

This house was built about 1841 by Welcome B. Lewis (1810-1880), a ship carpenter who often worked at the George Greenman & Co. Shipyard. Originally sided with clapboards and painted white, the house was built in the Greek Revival style then prevalent in the U.S.

The Lewis House has been used as a dormitory for the Williams College-Mystic Seaport Maritime Studies Program, a semester-long undergraduate program in American maritime history, literature, marine policy, and science. It is now used as offices by Mystic Seaport.

DICKERMAN HOUSE

This stucco house was built around 1900 for managers of the Rossie Velvet Company. The Museum purchased the building in 1968 and turned it into office space. It is named for Marion Dickerman, a noted educator and friend of Eleanor Roosevelt, who served as the Museum's director of educational programming from 1946 to 1962.

ART AND CUSTOM FRAMING GALLERY

This simple building was constructed in 1920 for Sebastiano Santin, an Italian immigrant who became a skilled automobile mechanic during the early years of the revolutionary shift to automobile transportation in the first third of the 1900s. His work was so much in demand that he opened this shop as Santin's Garage, Mystic's first automobile repair business. He soon prospered and opened in the same building the first local automobile dealership. Mr. Santin and his son Joseph sold Star, Durant, Flint, Studebaker, Chevrolet, and Oldsmobile cars here from 1920 to 1938, when the business outgrew this building and moved elsewhere.

The Santin family retained ownership and rented this building to other auto mechanics until 1950, when it was finally sold out of the family. That year the garage doors were sided over and the structure was

Restoring an Aquatic Environment

The pond next to the Art and Custom Framing Gallery does not look special, but it is especially significant. During the redesign of its parking lots, the Museum redesigned the adjoining wetlands. Opposite the main entrance, a small tidal marsh was rebuilt with plantings native to Connecticut salt marshes. This freshwater pond covers part of the site of a pasture pond in Greenmanville. It has been reshaped and replanted with native species to filter the storm water that runs off the nearby mill roof and parking lot, delivering clean water to the Mystic River. From bacteria to birds, it has become a little preserve of local nature. In summer you may see a "fountain" in the pond, which is an aerator to ensure that the water is well oxygenated so the pond can perform its purifying function.

converted into the Gingham Gate fabric shop, became a commercial landmark for residents and visitors alike for more than 40 years. From 1997 until its sale to Mystic Seaport in 2000, this building housed a Christmas shop. After a major rebuilding and remodeling, the building was reopened by the Museum as the Mystic Seaport Art and Custom Framing Gallery in 2001.

COLLECTIONS RESEARCH CENTER

When the McKinley Tariff of 1890 imposed a high duty on goods imported into the U.S., three German brothers named Rossie built a factory here to produce high-quality velvet. They opened the Rossie Velvet Company in 1898. Many German immigrants, including skilled velvet workers, moved to Mystic to work in the mill. They brought a German social and cultural flavor to this formerly Yankee shipbuilding and woolen-mill community. For decades, the Rossie Mill was Mystic's largest employer.

The original 150-by-60-foot building is the northwest portion of the present structure, along Greenmanville Avenue (Route 27). Five additions between 1902 and 1932 enlarged the building to its present size of 153,000 square feet, or 3.5 acres.

At its peak, the mill employed more than 200 workers, operating 150 looms. The work was hard, noisy, and repetitive, but a skilled craftsman, such as a loom fixer, could earn respectable wages. According to a former employee, the Rossie Velvet Company was "a nice place to work." Annual company outings and picnics suggest a community spirit within the mill.

The velvet mill remained in operation until

1958. By then, cheaper labor in the South made it hard for New England textile mills to compete. The machinery and fixtures were shipped to South Carolina to resume operation there. When the J. Rossie Velvet Company was dissolved in 1965, the building was leased to a number of enterprises before Mystic Seaport acquired it in 1973. As part of the Museum's renovation of the mill, the huge steam boilers were removed. The saw-tooth roof, which was designed to shed north light on the working floor, leaked from the beginning. It has been replaced, although the building facade was saved in the effort to give this mill a new life as a modern research and collections storage facility for Mystic Seaport.

The Collections Research Center opened in 2001. Although it is not open for casual visitation, researchers and visitors who need information or access to specific parts of the collections are welcome to contact the appropriate office to schedule a visit.

The Collections Research Center currently houses the following offices.

CURATORIAL DEPARTMENT

Simply put, the Curatorial Department cares for the objects in The Museum's collections. The curators are responsible for acquiring additions to the collections through donations or purchase. In the Registrar's Office, new objects are cataloged and the information is added to the permanent records on all the Museum's artifacts, which are maintained there. The curatorial storage and restoration staff oversees the collections. About one quarter of the Museum's objects are on exhibit. The rest are in storage, mostly in the new compact storage facility in the Collections Research Center, under proper temperature and humidity conditions for preservation. Most of the Museum's more than 500 watercraft are also in storage, and the Museum is planning a way to make this collection more accessible.

DANIEL S. GREGORY SHIPS PLANS LIBRARY

The Ships Plans Library, a division of the G.W. Blunt White Library, houses a major collection documenting the history of American naval architecture. With holdings of well over 100,000 sheets of plans plus 86 gore books and bound volumes, the collection includes plans for a wide variety of watercraft from the 1800s and 1900s, from rowing craft to sailboats, from steam yachts to fishing draggers. Many prominent designers and builders have donated their plans to Mystic Seaport, understanding that their work will be preserved and made accessible to scholars, boatbuilders, and dreamers alike.

PHOTOGRAPHY & LICENSING DEPARTMENT

The Photography & Licensing Department has three responsibilities: acquiring, preserving, and making accessible the Museum's historic photography and film and video collections; providing photographic services throughout the Museum and for outside clients; and managing the licensing and protection of the Museum's intellectual property.

The Historic Photography Collection is the largest maritime photographic archive in the United States, containing over 300,000 images from the 1840s to the present, spanning a wide range of commercial and recreational maritime activity, from New England shipbuilding to Arctic exploration.

The Rosenfeld Collection is the largest single collection of maritime photography in the world, consisting of over 800,000 images from the 1880s to the 1990s, and includes three generations of Rosenfeld work emphasizing yachting and boating, but also including naval and commercial images.

The Contemporary Photo Archive contains documentary photography of our vessels and historic buildings, loaned historic photos relating to research projects, and current images of Mystic Seaport for Museum use and licensing purposes.

In the new photography studio and laboratory, the Museum's photographers shoot and process both film and digital photography.

The Licensing Office expands awareness of the Museum's collections through licensing and product development, and also protects the Museum's intellectual property against unauthorized exploitation and trademark infringement.

FILM & VIDEO DIVISION

The Film & Video Division of the Photography Department contains both an archive and a production facility. The Film & Video Archive consists of 200 Film & Video Collections containing over 1.5 million feet of film and 5,000 videotapes of maritime subjects kept in proper cold storage. The division also documents Museum activities, serves the needs of documentary and commercial film and video producers, and produces informational programming for the Museum.

PUBLICATIONS DEPARTMENT & PRODUCT DEVELOPMENT DIVISION

As a central part of its educational mission, Mystic Seaport has been publishing monographs since 1930 and trade books since 1970. The Publications Department oversees the acquisition, editing, and production of books.

The Product Development Division is responsible for the development, production, management, and support of wholesale and retail products related to Mystic Seaport's collections and mission. Products range from fine art and photographic prints to ceramics, glassware, and textiles. The Product Development Division also works with the Licensing Office to assure quality standards of Museum products produced by outside vendors.

SHOPPING AT MYSTIC SEAPORT

Mystic Seaport Stores

Mystic Seaport's shops are a destination in and of themselves. At the *Museum Store*, just outside the Museum's main entrance, you'll find more than 8,300 square feet and two floors filled with reproductions from our collections, select photography from the renowned *Rosenfeld Collection*, unique seafaring gifts, toys, model

ships, prints, and posters. Upstairs, our bookstore offers more than 90 of Mystic Seaport's published titles, as well as rare volumes and the nation's most complete selection of maritime books. After your visit you can still shop at Mystic Seaport Stores on the Web at www.mysticseaportstores.org

THE MARITIME GALLERY AT MYSTIC SEAPORT

You'll have even more to browse in our Schaefer *Maritime Gallery*, the nation's premier gallery specializing in contemporary marine art and ship models. Working closely with the world's finest marine artists, the Gallery offers some of the best work on the market, including hundreds of paintings, models, sculptures, and scrimshaw. Collectors can also find several major theme exhibitions each year.

MYSTIC SEAPORT ART & CUSTOM FRAMING GALLERY

Once you've found the perfect painting or print, bring it over to the *Art and Custom Framing Gallery*, offering a huge selection of prints and posters, as well as one of the largest displays of preframed art in Southeastern Connecticut. Our expert staff, with more than 40 years of combined framing experience, will help you find the perfect match for your piece.

If you're planning on visiting our shops, don't forget to consider a Mystic Seaport *membership*, which can provide significant discounts on our merchandise.

EATING AT MYSTIC SEAPORT

At Mystic Seaport, experience the life of a sailor, not the meals. As much as we love authentic seafaring experiences, we just can't bring ourselves to serve our visitors stale bread and water. That's why we offer dozens of delicious alternatives at Mystic Seaport's dining venues.

THE SEAMEN'S INNE RESTAURANT & PUB

The *Seamen's Inne Restaurant & Pub* is a Connecticut landmark, serving lunch, dinner, and Sunday brunch. You can also grab a drink or a bite to eat in our cozy pub. In warmer weather, eat outside on the patio.

SCHAEFER'S SPOUTER TAVERN

If you work up a thirst or an appetite strolling the Museum streets, step into *Schaefer's Spouter Tavern* for the feel and flavor of a waterfront tavern. The tavern's name honors Ishmael's "very spot for cheap lodging" described in *Moby-Dick*. It is open in the warmer months and offers simple fare, served by costumed staff.

THE GALLEY

If you're looking for something a little more quick and casual, check out the *Galley Restaurant.* With informal tray service and a convenient location just inside the Museum's main entrance, this is the place to meet up with friends and family and grab breakfast, or a lunch of sandwiches, fish and chips, burgers, and traditional sodas.

STREET VENDORS

In a seaport in the 1800s, you would find street vendors hawking all sorts of hand food and drink for workers and passersby. At Mystic Seaport, in warm weather you'll find costumed staff throughout our grounds, serving authentic treats like iced traditional sodas and lemonade, homemade pickles, ice cream, and cookies. Get into the spirit, grab a bite, and relax on one of our shaded benches.

MEMBERSHIP

If you're enjoying your visit, think of joining our family. Since its establishment more than 75 years ago, Mystic Seaport has been a nonprofit membership organization. The Museum now has more than 22,000 members from all 50 states and 38 foreign countries. When you become a member of Mystic Seaport, you are supporting the country's leading maritime museum. Whether you take advantage of the unlimited free admission or simply enjoy receiving our member newsletter, the *Wind Rose*, your membership makes you part of the Mystic Seaport family.

Besides free admission, membership in the Museum offers you opportunities to participate in special programs at the Museum, travel with other Museum members, receive discounts on programs, classes, and merchandise, and purchase members-only clothing and gifts.

New members are encouraged to pick up their copy of the *Wind Rose* to find out about coming events for the entire Museum. There, you'll find out about all of the exciting and educational programs we offer exclusively to our members and their guests.

As a Member, come relax and mingle in the comfort of the Membership Building. You can enjoy a complimentary cup of coffee, tea, hot chocolate, or lemonade while browsing through the latest magazines, or playing a game of checkers. Our bookshelves are full of books related to the sea, and our restrooms are away from the bustle of visitors. Our private member's terrace, behind the Membership Building, is available for picnics or quiet contemplation.

Information on membership categories is available at the admission gate, at the Membership Building and other locations on the grounds, or at the Museum's Web site, www.mysticseaport.org.

So whether you visit often or support the Museum from a distance, membership in Mystic Seaport is a beneficial way to help the cause of maritime preservation while increasing your own enjoyment of this very special place.

WHAT ELSE CAN WE DO?

Whether it's testing your luck at Foxwoods Resort Casino or Mohegan Sun, bonding with Mystic Aquarium's Beluga whales, touring a New England winery, experiencing art, or simply spending a day at a luxury spa—whatever escape you crave at whatever speed you seek, you can find it in Mystic Places.

From nightclubs and entertainment to quaint village streets, from sunset sails to popular attractions, Mystic Places is home to a year-round array of unexpected and easy-to-reach discoveries.

Spend time in a place that has been treasured for centuries by sea captains and artists and today by city dwellers and families seeking inspiration, relaxation, and an opportunity to recharge.

COME LEARN WITH US

As a nonprofit educational institution, Mystic Seaport is here to help people learn. During your visit, you participated in many informal learning programs amid the exhibits.

In summer, kids enroll in day-camp programs at the Museum. Teenagers can spend a week living on the *Joseph Conrad* and learning to sail or sailing along the coast as part of the crew of the schooner *Brilliant.* In spring and fall there are sailing programs for both youths and adults.

Throughout the year, the Museum offers courses in various aspects of boatbuilding. The Planetarium offers courses on navigation and weather. A variety of evening courses are offered in the village exhibits, including blacksmithing and hearth cooking.

School programs include in-school presentations, day visits, and specialized overnight programs. For college undergraduates, the semester-long Williams College-Mystic Seaport Maritime Studies Program offers intensive study in history, literature, and marine science, with travels afield and to sea. Graduate students can participate in the summer Munson Institute of American Maritime Studies.

The Paul Cuffe Memorial Fellowship supports research in the history of Native and African Americans in coastal southern New England. Those pursuing their own learning projects are welcome at the Museum's research library or, by appointment, to inspect artifacts in storage.

Whether you live nearby or far away, we invite you to come learn at Mystic Seaport. Check the Museum's Web site—www.mysticseaport.org—for details.

If You Want to Know More

Mystic Seaport has published more than 90 books on American maritime history subjects. The following books, videos, and CDs relate to the Museum and its exhibits.

Maritime History
Robert G. Albion, et al., *New England and the Sea* (revised, 1994)
Andrew W. German, *Voyages: Stories of America and the Sea* (2000)
Benjamin W. Labaree, et al., *America and the Sea: A Maritime History* (1998)
John F. Leavitt, *Wake of the Coasters* (revised, 1984)

Mystic Seaport
Waldo Howland, *Integrity: A Life in Boats* vol. 3 (2004)
Mystic Seaport Coloring Book (2000)
Sandra L. Oliver, *Saltwater Foodways* (1995)

Mystic Seaport Vessels
Maynard Bray, et al., *Mystic Seaport Watercraft* (revised, 2001)
Anne and Maynard Bray, *Boat Plans at Mystic Seaport* (2000)
Flagships of Mystic Seaport (2000)
Benjamin A.G. Fuller, *87 Boat Designs* (2002)

Analuisa
Eric P. Roorda, *Analuisa: Cuba, America and the Sea* (2005)

Breck Marshall
Barry Thomas, *Building the Crosby Catboat* (1989)

Brilliant
Philip Gerard, *Brilliant Passage* (1989)
George Moffett, *Aboard an American Classic* (2002)
Mystic Seaport Video Postcard: The *Brilliant* collection

Charles W. Morgan
Nelson C. Haley, *Whale Hunt* (revised, 1990)
John F. Leavitt, *The Charles W. Morgan* (revised, 1998)
On board the Morgan, video (1990)
Charles W. Morgan: Voyages of the Past, Present & Future, video CD Rom

L.A. Dunton
W.M.P. Dunne, *Thomas McManus and the American Fishing Schooner* (1994)

Joseph Conrad
Alan Villiers, *Joey Goes to Sea* (2005)

Sabino
George King III, *A Steamboat Named Sabino* (1999)

Whaleboats
Willits D. Ansel, *The Whaleboat* (revised, 1983)

Astronomy and Navigation
Reach for the Sky activity kit
Sundial Kit
Susan P. Howell, *Practical Celestial Navigation* (1993)

Figureheads
Georgia Hamilton, *Silent Pilots* (1984)

Paintings and Photography
The Art of the Boat (2005)
Dorothy E.R. Brewington, *Marine Paintings and Drawings in Mystic Seaport Museum* (1982)
Stanley Rosenfeld, *A Century Under Sail* (1988)
Stanley Rosenfeld, *A Point of View* (2005)
John Rousmaniere, *Sleek* (2003)

Sea Music
Annual Sea Music Festival CDs
Frederick P. Harlow, *Chanteying Aboard American Ships* (2004)
Stan Hugill, *Shanties from the Seven Seas* (1994)
Gale Huntington, *Songs the Whalemen Sang* (2005)
Songs of the Sailor Songbook (1998)

TAKE A VOYAGE

Be the Captain, Go on a Virtual Tour, Play Some Games to Test Your Skills of Seamanship, Read a Story, Watch Some Historic Video Footage, Listen to Some Music the Seamen Sang

INTERACTIVE MULTIMEDIA CD-ROM

Mac & PC
COMPATIBLE

CHARLES W. MORGAN

Voyages of the Past, Present & Future

HISTORIC VIDEO CLIPS • 3-D VIRTUAL-TOURS • SHIP'S PLANS
NARRATION BY PHIL CUTTING • PHOTOS
INTERACTIVE GAMES • ORIGINAL MUSIC • WEB LINKS

MYSTIC SEAPORT   THE MUSEUM OF AMERICA AND THE SEA™

1033798 $19.95

MYSTIC SEAPORT®, The Museum of America and the Sea, has compiled this interactive, multimedia CD-Rom in celebration of the *Charles W. Morgan*, America's last wooden whaling ship. You can go aboard the *Morgan* and tour the entire ship. Historic footage shows what it was like to sail aboard a wooden whaleship. Historic and present day photos as well as narrated stories bring the experience to life on your computer screen.

Five activities make your travels fun and challenging. History has been made accessible and fun.

For more information or to order contact:

MYSTIC SEAPORT STORES
860.572.5386
800.331.2665
www.mysticseaport.org/stores

Some of the new
books published by
MYSTIC SEAPORT

*The Marine Art of
Geoff Hunt*
ISBN 0-939511-00-2
1031537
$45.00

Joey Goes to Sea
ISBN 0-939511-10-X
1036513
$9.95

*Folklore
and the Sea*
ISBN
0-913372-36-6
1011319
$24.95

*Album of American
Traditions*
ISBN 0-939510-95-2
1032020
$50.00

OUR PRODUCT IS ALL ABOUT NAUTICAL.

Silk Ties inspired from artists Jeffrey Sabol and Randall Enos
a. 7592110 (navy) $36.00 b. 7592210 (maroon) $36.00
c. 7592310 (olive) $36.00 d. 7591910 (New Bedford Boys) $26.95
e. 7591810 (whaling) $26.95 f. 7592010 (sunset) $36.00

THE ROSENFELD LIBRARY

SAILS & SAILING
Franco Giorgetti
ISBN 0-913372-88-9
1011312 $50.00

A CENTURY UNDER SAIL
Text by Stanley Rosenfeld
ISBN 0-939510-71-5
1015387 $50.00

A CENTURY
Under Sail

SELECTED PHOTOGRAPHS BY *Morris Rosenfeld and Stanley*
legendary photographers of the America's Cup races

Text by Stanley Rosenfeld

SAILS & SAILING

MYSTIC SEAPORT

Sleek

CLASSIC IMAGES FROM THE
ROSENFELD COLLECTION

SLEEK
John Rousmaniere
ISBN 0-939510-90-1
1026230 $50.00

25th Annual Sea Music Festival
CD 1036189 $14.95

NAUTICAL TRIVIA
• The Sailing Board Game •

Take the
TRIVIA CHALLENGE ...

Nautical Trivia
1033342 $50.00